Herbert Smith Freehills Kramer
PORTRAIT AWARD 2025

NATIONAL PORTRAIT GALLERY

Contents

Director's Foreword

In our annual celebration of portrait paintings, the *Herbert Smith Freehills Kramer Portrait Award* showcases the work of artists working today all over the world. This year marks the second presentation of the Award following the Gallery's reopening in 2023, and we are so grateful for the support of our sponsors, Herbert Smith Freehills Kramer, which allows for the continuation of free access to this exhibition.

This year, we received 1,314 entries from 61 countries – an astonishing number and range of painted portraits. The judging panel viewed 274 of these works in person and had the challenging task of selecting just 46 for the final presentation at the National Portrait Gallery. These 46 works display an engaging spectrum of approaches to portraiture, with a mix of classic and contemporary stylistic choices, demonstrating the abundance of talent of artists working in this genre around the world.

The artworks in this year's exhibition largely explore relationships, both social and familial. With an increased focus on the connection between the artist and sitter, the personal stories of how the portraits came to be are fascinating in themselves: artists painting their children, sitters returning the favour, or even chance encounters that developed into deep friendships.

I would like to warmly congratulate Moira Cameron on being awarded First Prize for *A Life Lived*. Cameron works with different oil paint textures to recreate a self-portrait from 40 years ago. Congratulations also go to Tim Benson and Martyn Harris who have been awarded Second and Third Prize respectively for their skilful portraits, which emphasise the importance of community; and to Michelle Liu who has been selected for this year's Young Artist Award for the very sensitively painted portrait, *Kofi*.

Thank you to the team at the National Portrait Gallery for their attentive and creative commitment to the Portrait Award – the process itself as well as the exhibition and publication. I am also grateful to the White Wall Company for their fantastic management of the judging process.

Finally, a big thank you this year's judges for their time and for their very thorough and insightful work on this selection: Professor Dorothy Price, Maggi Hambling, Peter Brathwaite, Rosie Broadley and panel chair Rosie Wilson.

Victoria Siddall
Director
National Portrait Gallery, London

Sponsor's Foreword

The prestigious *Herbert Smith Freehills Kramer Portrait Award* is a platform from which many portrait artists hope to launch or expand their career. The Award – amongst the most important in the art world – encourages established artists, and the next generation, to share their outstanding talent with art lovers.

Herbert Smith Freehills Kramer are delighted to continue supporting the National Portrait Gallery, as we have since 2004, in our second year in sponsorship of the Portrait Award. We are proud that our collaboration ensures that the renowned and global competition continues to grow, and allows incredible works of art to be freely accessed by hundreds of thousands of people every year in a beautifully curated exhibition.

This year, the Award received entries from 61 different countries. The breadth of perspectives and approaches that this brings to the Award is incredibly important, with portraits able to tell a story otherwise untold. The judges sifted through over a thousand artworks, embedded with stories and narratives that reveal the lived experience of individuals from around the globe. With the final 46 works on display, meticulously selected by the judges, the exhibition is a showcase of artistic variety all connected by human experience.

I truly value our enduring relationship and connection with the National Portrait Gallery and this fantastic Award and exhibition, promoting artists from all backgrounds. I hope that the visitors to this exhibition will enjoy the final selection of works. I send warm congratulations to each exhibition artist on their inspirational pieces.

Justin D'Agostino MH
Global CEO
Herbert Smith Freehills Kramer

The Judges

Peter Brathwaite
Opera Singer, Artist, and Writer

As a performer, I am captivated by vivid storytelling and urgent narratives that encourage us to question our perspectives and think differently. It was exhilarating to serve on the judging panel and engage with portraits that do just that. From emphatic statement pieces to intimate, contemplative reflections, these works speak to the beauty of individuality while also addressing our shared concerns.

Maggi Hambling
Artist

On entering the vast building, an overwhelming army of portraits advanced upon us. Daunting. I searched for real intensity of response from the artist to the subject. In the four prizewinners I found it.

Rosie Wilson
Director of Programmes, Partnerships and Collections, National Portrait Gallery

I greatly enjoyed chairing the judging for this year's Portrait Award – it was an inspiring day for me. It was wonderful to see the variety of portraits being produced by artists at home and internationally. The engaging conversations amongst the judging panel, and thoughtful consideration of the works, resulted in a beautiful selection and final exhibition.

Rosie Broadley
Senior Curator of 20th Century Collections, National Portrait Gallery

Judging the Portrait Award was a great privilege and a huge challenge, as each entry represents so much hard work and hope. I was grateful to share the responsibility with my fellow judges who brought such valuable insight to the process. Looking for a sense of connection between the artist and sitter, I was particularly struck by the joy and tenderness represented in the submissions.

Professor Dorothy Price FBA
Art Historian and Academic, The Courtauld Institute of Art

It was an honour to be a judge of the Portrait Award this year. My fellow judges and I had a thoroughly enjoyable and challenging day assessing such interesting works. It was difficult to choose one over another, but we were unanimous in our final selection and hope that visitors enjoy the works as much as we did. Congratulations to those who submitted, keep painting!

The Prizes

First Prize

Moira Cameron

Cameron utilises gestural, expressive brushstrokes to reference and reignite a previous self-portrait from 40 years prior (p.8).

Second Prize

Tim Benson

Thick brushstrokes and a limited palette contribute to Benson's depiction of an important community figure, while championing the beauty of facial difference (p.10).

Third Prize

Martyn Harris

Harris captures a quiet moment of wistful reflection of his dear friend, over the course of three sittings (p.12).

Young Artist Award

Michelle Liu

Depicting a friend, Liu seeks to create a depth of connection between the sitter and viewer that transcends the boundary of the canvas (p.14).

The *Herbert Smith Freehills Kramer Portrait Award* is open to artists from around the world, aged 18 or over. Exhibited annually at the National Portrait Gallery, London, the Award showcases talented artists, both professional and amateur. The winner of the competition receives £35,000, with second prize receiving £12,000 and third prize £10,000. The Young Artist Award winner, aged between 18 and 30, receives £9,000.

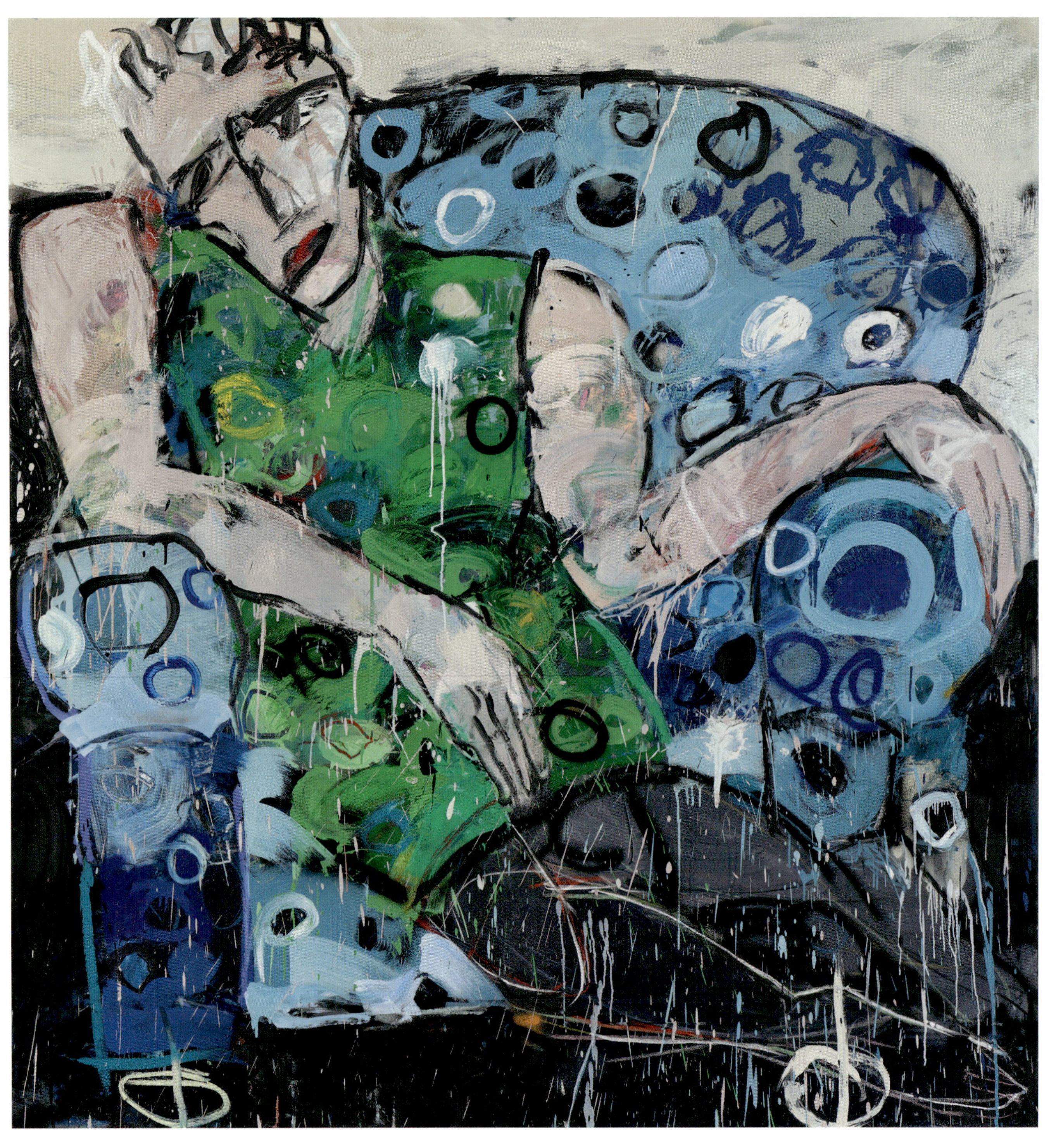

Moira Cameron
A Life Lived, 2024
Oil on canvas
2200 × 2000mm

First Prize
Moira Cameron

Born in London into a family of sculptors and painters, Moira Cameron's artistic calling was never in question. 'Art runs in my blood. My grandmother, mother, father, and sister were all trained artists. I married an artist, and our son is one too,' she says. 'As a child, equipment was always at hand, and drawing was encouraged. I was fully immersed in the visual world my family created around me.'

Cameron met her husband, Pop artist David Spiller, while studying at Ravensbourne Art College, London, in the 1980s. Relocating to New York City, she made text and graffiti works, repurposing paper grocery bags with spray-painted slogans and song lyrics. As Spiller gained recognition and the couple then began a family in the United Kingdom, Cameron set aside her own artistic pursuits to support him and they worked together until his death in 2018.

Cameron has since partnered with her artist son, Xavier, under the name Spiller+Cameron. Their work exhibits a series of mixed-media collages in which their individual paintings are cut up, recomposed and sewn back together in a 'deeply entwined' creative process. Now, following her son's recent move to the United States to pursue a solo career, and his encouragement for his mother to 'start afresh', Cameron has finally returned to her own practice after decades of collaboration. 'It is the beginning of a new chapter,' she says. 'A reinvention.'

As part of this newfound independence, Cameron is reimagining paintings she created as a student 40 years ago, inspired by a visit to the National Gallery's *Van Gogh: Poets and Lovers* exhibition, London, 2024. There, she was reminded of the freedom in Van Gogh's painting and drawn in particular to two portraits of Arles cafe owner Madame Ginoux: *L'Arlésienne (Portrait of Madame Ginoux)* (1890) and *L'Arlésienne (The Woman from Arles)* (1890), each depicting the same sitter but carrying a 'different presence'.

This idea of revisiting the same subject with varied interpretations underpins Cameron's current work. Her winning entry in the 2025 Portrait Award, *A Life Lived*, is an evolution of a self-portrait she made at art college in 1982 titled *The Green Dress*. It no longer exists, so Cameron used a photograph of the piece as reference, working in 'intense, frenzied bursts' at her high-ceilinged studio near London's Oval to capture the energy of the original. 'As a student, I painted voraciously, never considering my works as precious or worth keeping. I documented each piece and moved on, without regret. Looking back at those records now evokes memories and connections to my younger self.'

Cameron began the new portrait by sketching the image with pastels and spray paint before applying thick layers of oil paint – brushed, palette-knifed, or smeared by hand – followed by more fluid oils. Some areas are scraped, washed away, and repainted, while others are intentionally left barely touched. 'The drips, for me, add movement and a sense of freedom – a return to painting purely for my own pleasure, without purpose or restraint.'

While *A Life Lived* mirrors the composition of the earlier work, it carries the weight of years. Here, we see an older woman who has lived, observed and felt deeply. 'My posture conveys quiet fatigue, shoulders slightly slumped, head tilted in reflection,' says Cameron. 'The lines on my face, the subtle shadows, tell a story of time passing, of laughter and worry, of a life fully experienced. It is more than a moment; it holds a lifetime within it.'

Interview by Richard McClure

Second Prize
Tim Benson

London-based Tim Benson attributes his lifelong passion for painting to his artist mother dragging him to nearby Kenwood House as a child to view Rembrandt's *Self-Portrait with Two Circles* (1665–69). It was this formative experience that sowed the seeds for an award-winning career that has yielded international commissions, a string of solo and group exhibitions and his present role as President of the Royal Institute of Oil Painters.

Training at art schools in Glasgow and London, Benson began as a landscape painter before switching his focus to figurative work. He uses the same rigorous observation and bold, impasto mark making to create pared back, frame-filling portraits that prize the sitter's character and story as much as the need for an absolute likeness.

'I am simply fascinated by the physicality of human heads, and never feel the need to use objects or symbols to add narrative to my portraits,' he explains. 'Ideally, a portrait will satisfy both the need for expression and precision, and must obtain a likeness. However, this does not come from a straight copy of the person in front of me. I tend to magnify the physical traits that instantly catch my attention. There is a degree of caricature; I always seek to make the sitter a slightly amplified version of themselves.'

Benson often collaborates with charities and NGOs to picture 'those whose voices are rarely heard', travelling to Sierra Leone, West Africa, in 2015 to paint and interview 40 Ebola survivors and the medics involved in containing the virus. The project culminated in an audio-visual exhibition at London's Mall Galleries. For an ongoing series that raises awareness of climate change, Benson has visited the Philippines to meet people living with rising sea levels: 'For me, portrait painting is about chronicling someone's experience,' he says. 'It is about storytelling.'

The subject of Benson's entry in the 2025 Portrait Award also has a story to tell. The artist first painted London outreach worker Cliff in 2019 as part of a series highlighting inspirational Haringey residents who serve the local community.

'I was drawn to Cliff's face and the important role that he provides in helping young people to start and grow businesses, so I was keen to paint him again. Cliff has a facial difference, which is as much part of his story as his work in the community. Painting him has afforded me the opportunity to challenge historical notions of beauty in portraiture whilst also advocating for the destigmatisation of facial difference.'

Benson typically paints from a single, four-hour sitting, but here the portrait was made from sketches and photographs taken in Cliff's office due to his subject's busy schedule. Working quickly with a limited palette, he paints straight to canvas with a wide, flat brush that prevents excessive detailing and allows him to 'sculpt' in thick oils with as few brush strokes as necessary.

'My work is never more than a couple of perilous brush marks away from falling into the realms of abstraction, and losing its representational foundation, but that is the knife-edge I seek to occupy as a painter,' he says. 'It is about immediacy and creating a dynamic interpretation of the sitter. First and foremost, a good portrait should have an emotive quality. If the painting does not engage the viewer then it is not doing its job.'

Interview by Richard McClure

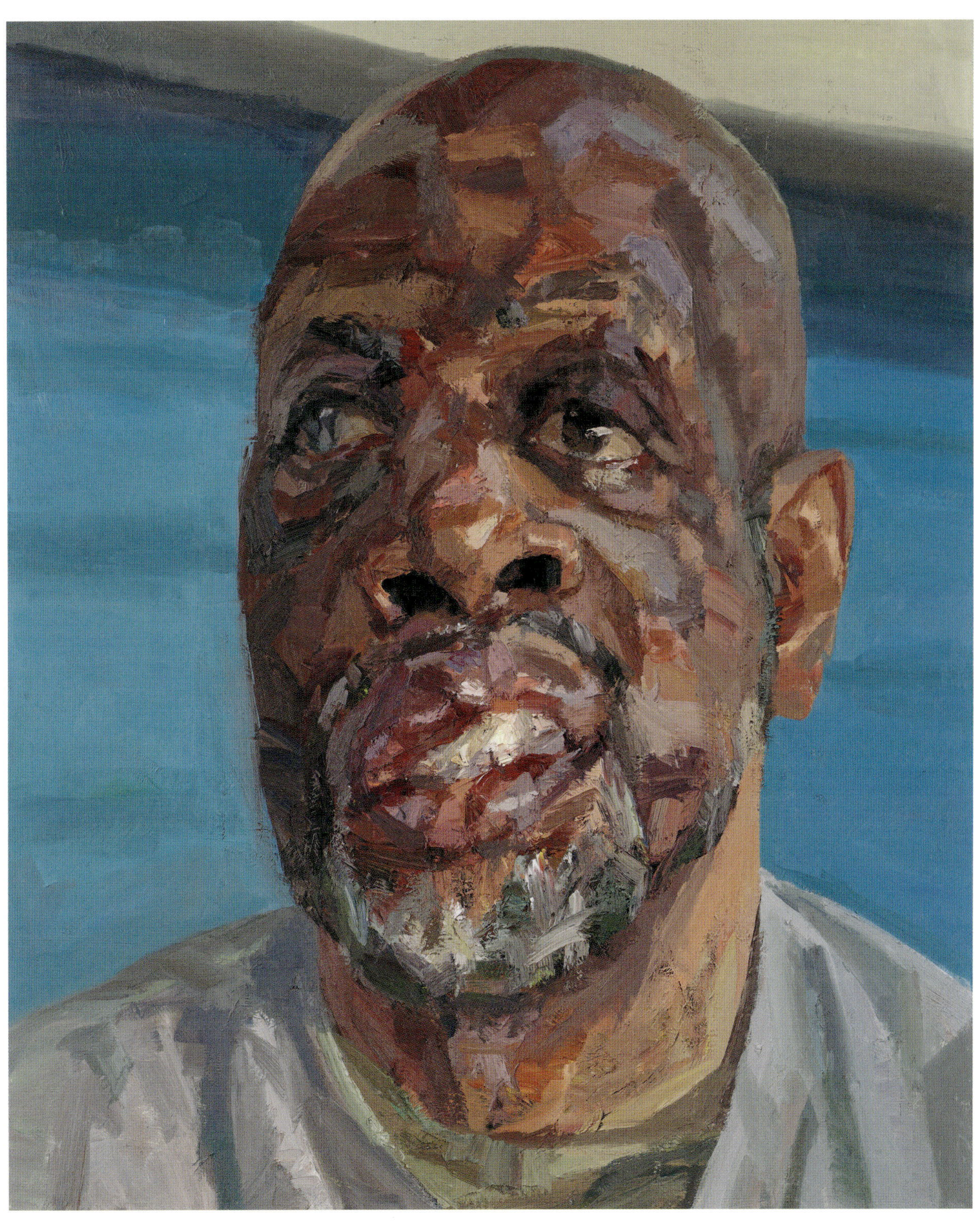

Tim Benson
Cliff, Outreach Worker, 2024
Oil on canvas
1520 × 1220mm

Third Prize
Martyn Harris

Martyn Harris set up as a full-time artist eight years ago, following a long and varied career that included jobs as a mechanical engineer and draughtsman. The meticulous and painstaking nature of his previous occupations can be detected in measured, closely observed portraits that have been selected several times for the Royal Society of Portrait Painters' annual exhibition, in London. 'It was always my dream to become an artist,' he says. 'Before I turned professional, I would often work through the night on my paintings, losing track of time. I finally feel that I am being true to myself.'

Among his influences is the Newlyn School, the colony of late nineteenth-century artists who recorded scenes of rural life in Cornwall. Harris' work is similarly rooted in place and time. Born in Halesowen, near Birmingham, Harris was mentored by local landscape painter WR Jennings, and now lives in the Black Country town of Cradley Heath where, as artist in residence at the Art Yard Gallery, his commissioned portraits illustrate a cross-section of West Midlands society, from charity volunteers to academics and dignitaries.

'What appeals to me most about the Newlyn School is their depiction of people in their everyday lives. There is an honesty to their work and a sensitivity that I try to emulate,' he notes. 'I have clients around the UK, but portraying my own community is very important to me.'

In 2023, he was awarded the Smallwood Architects Prize for his study of a local antiques dealer seated among the quirky treasures of his bric-a-brac emporium, while his prizewinning entry in the 2025 Portrait Award also depicts a Cradley Heath resident. When painting in his studio, he would often notice an elderly woman who visited the gallery to pass the afternoon. Striking up a friendship, and moved by her 'vulnerability and introspective expression',

he asked if she would sit for a portrait, one that would reflect on the passage of time and the fragility of ageing.

'Gillian and I have become close friends and often sit and chat about the arts and life in general,' he says. 'I chose the title *Memories* to show where she is in her life. Her arthritic hands are clasped together as if in contemplation or quiet resignation, and the viewer is invited to consider what Gillian has lived through. What thoughts occupy her mind? Is she reminiscing about the past or contemplating her future?'

Beginning with a charcoal drawing, the creative process involved three sittings. Harris then spent six weeks building up several glazes to achieve the translucent skin tones, working from photographic references and painting on panel for greater precision. 'What I love about panels is that every stroke is visible, whereas on canvas the weave absorbs some of the brushwork,' he explains. 'I am a realist painter and achieving a true and precise likeness is very important to me, but I try not to be ruled by a photographic image, and always explore where the portrait can be abstracted.'

Gillian was a guest when the portrait was unveiled by the Royal Birmingham Society of Artists last year, and though the image touches upon themes of loneliness, sorrow and the weight of time, both artist and sitter found their collaboration uplifting: 'Gillian has enjoyed the whole experience,' says Harris. 'She has even become something of a local celebrity.'

Interview by Richard McClure

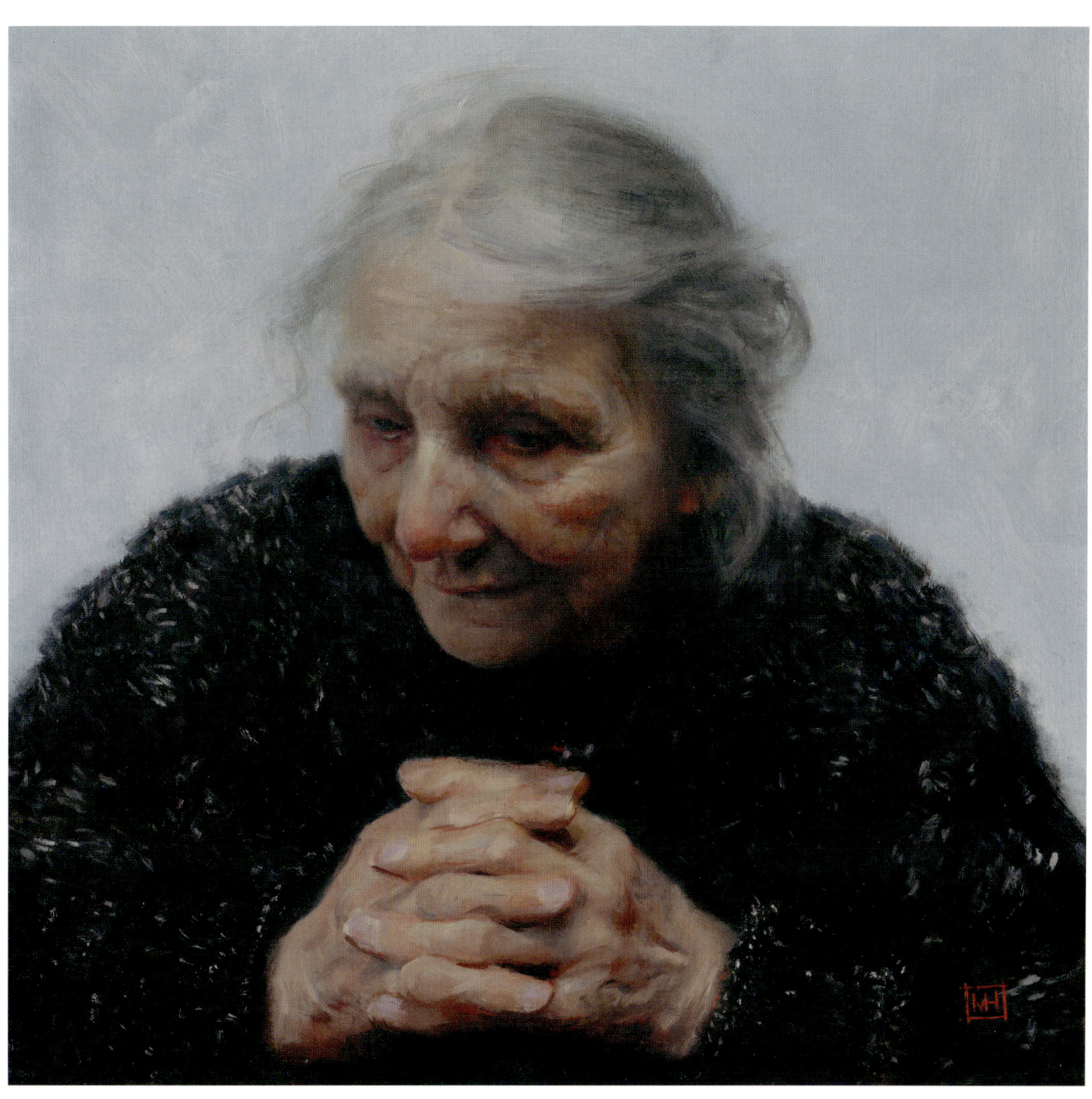

Martyn Harris
Memories, 2024
Oil on board
400 × 400mm

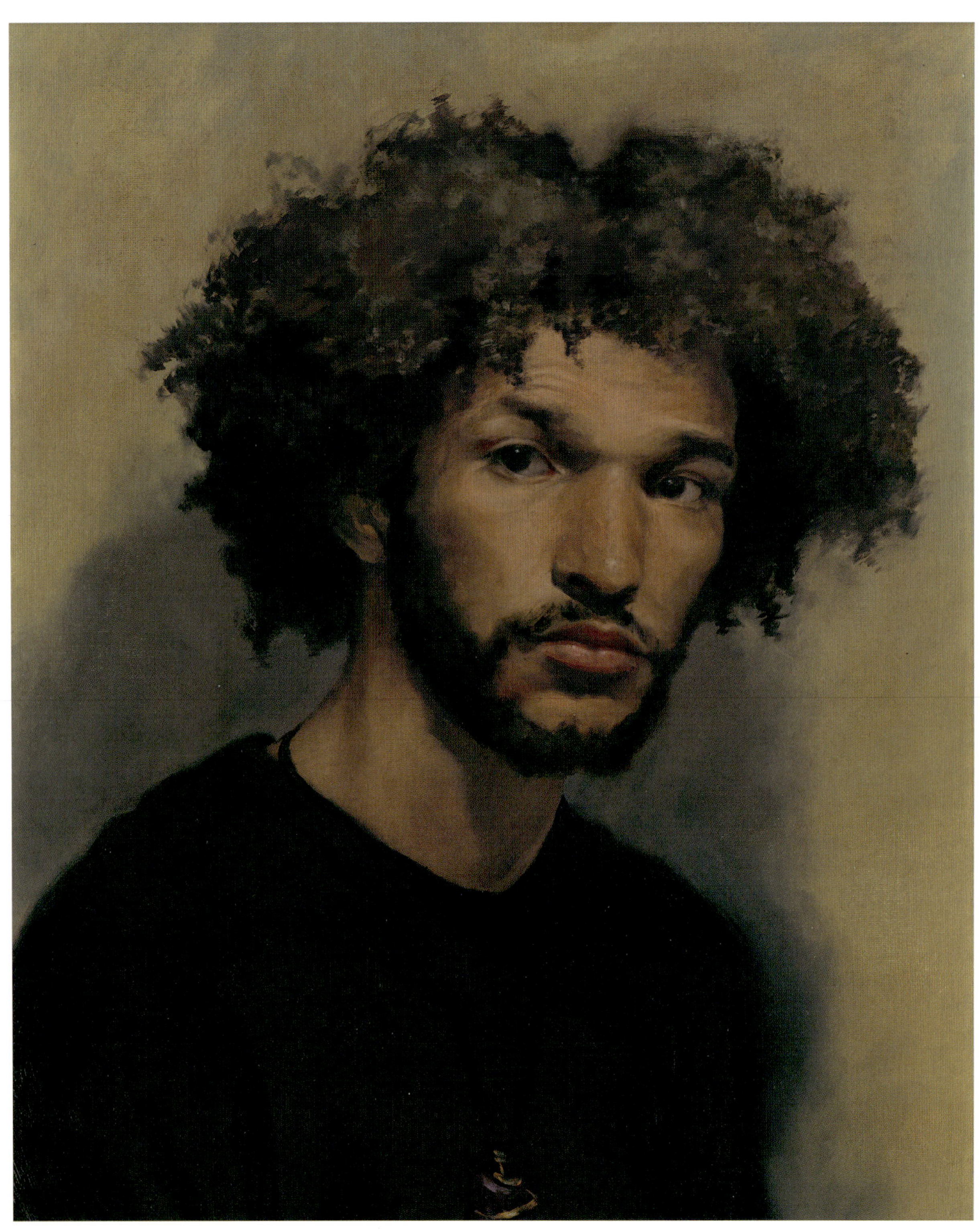

Michelle Liu
Kofi, 2024
Oil on canvas
500 × 400mm

Young Artist Award Michelle Liu

Michelle Liu was born in El Segundo, California, and has spent most of her adult life in New York City. Three years ago, she relocated to London, England, to work for tech giant Google as a Customer Engineer, providing clients with solutions and strategies. As a consequence, her artistic endeavours are confined to evenings and weekends. 'I am lucky and enjoy what I do for work, but there is a deep focus and tactility that comes with art, which is a great foil to my day job,' she says. 'There is a problem solving aspect that is common to both. The process of making art can be quite technical and structured. A painting is like a hundred puzzles in one.'

As a teenager, Liu was introduced to the principles of classical art at Otis College of Art and Design in Los Angeles, and is now a long-distance member of the Salmagundi Club, a New York City exhibition and meeting space for representational artists. In London, she can often be found sketching at museums and galleries, honing her charcoal skills by copying masterworks by artists such as John Singer Sargent. 'Even if my paintings have a loose look to them, it is critical that the structural integrity of the drawing is there,' she explains. 'Sargent has taught me that you do not have to sacrifice realism for impressionism, and I try to incorporate certain techniques of his to achieve a similar impact.'

Liu has received the Young Artist Award for her entry, *Kofi*, which was completed at Big Turtle Studio in south London. Her subject, an occasional life model and friend of the studio owners, sparked Liu's imagination with both his 'aloof slouch' and expressive brow bone; she painted him alongside several other artists of various skill levels, over three Saturday drop-in sessions. The communal arrangement meant that Liu was unable to direct most aspects of the sitting, though she believes the advantages of painting in a group outweigh the drawbacks.

'My progress has come on in leaps and bounds since I have had a community of artists around me to share techniques, tips and critiques,' she says. 'I actually prefer to work within the constraints of time, my position to the model, or the studio environment, because it forces you to have a clear plan of attack. Even if you end up outside of your comfort zone, it is a great way to experiment. For the portrait of Kofi, I was concerned about the yellow lighting in the studio, but it actually translated into a really nice glow.'

Liu, who has exhibited at London's Wimbledon Art Fair and the Chelsea Art Society, begins her portraits with a thin monochrome underpainting, establishing the shape, design and overall colour washes, before layering more paint *alla prima* – where paint is applied wet-on-wet. Painting from life is an integral part of Liu's practice. She prefers to work without photo references, believing their use can leave the portrait flat and spiritless.

'My portraiture has evolved over time, having gone through a period of leaving them a bit unfinished, but with *Kofi* I wanted to develop the picture further,' she says. 'I am happy with the balance of detail and looseness. The black shirt and necklace are only a few brush strokes, but placed correctly, whereas the detail of the slight eyebrow raise and few defined curls of hair do not distract from the overall portrait. It is about capturing all the imperceptible shifts of the model as a single cohesive picture. The values of the entire portrait need to work in harmony.'

Interview by Richard McClure

Exhibitors

Tallulah Hutson
Waiting in Shade, 2024
Oil on canvas
1800 × 1800mm

Tallulah Hutson's *Waiting in Shade* is central to a series of works exploring ideas of vulnerability and challenging traditional notions of masculinity. The pressures of gender expectations are visualised in this large portrait through a pervasive and persistent uncertainty. Tensions travel across the canvas, and manifest in a series of internal contradictions: between the face and the pose, the flowers and the sitter's boots, the light and the darkness.

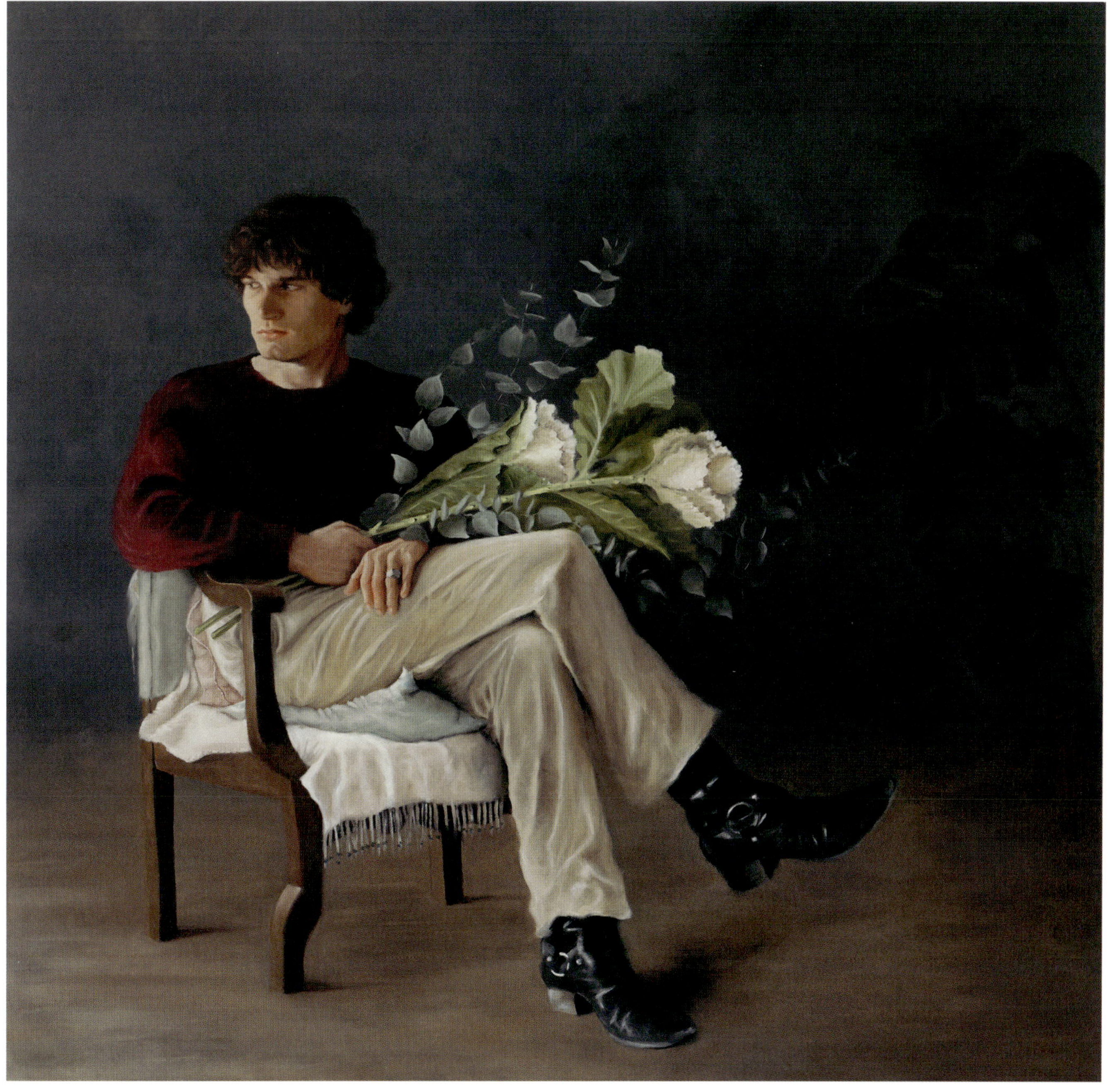

Yvadney Davis
Inset Day, 2025
Oil and acrylic on canvas
1200 × 1000mm

A familiar domestic scene is the basis for Yvadney Davis'
compelling exploration of mother-daughter relationships.
Inset Day captures 'the duality of our emotions caught
between love, duty and a need for space'. With a mischievous
energy, the artist's daughter scrambles over cushions on
the back of a sofa. Davis, sat brightly dressed but weary,
holds a strong gaze that confronts the viewer, expressing
the weight of motherhood as imperative to, yet distinct
from, the freedom of childhood.

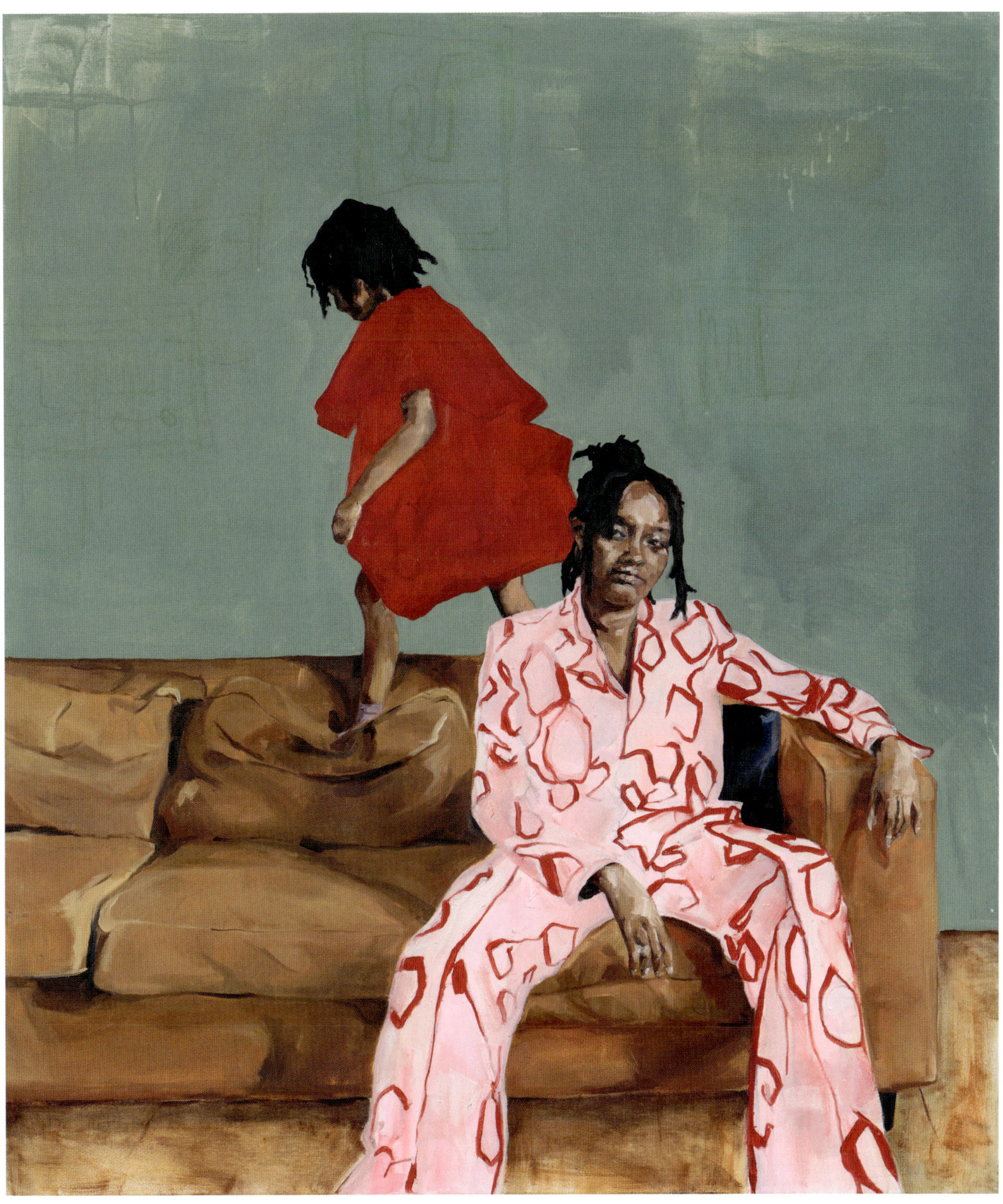

Paul Wright
Smaller World, 2025
Oil on canvas
1350 × 1300mm

Paul Wright's portrait represents his 81-year-old mother
who suffers from Alzheimer's disease. Dressed in blue
with a book resting on her knee, Patricia is fixed at the
centre of a swirl of half-formed objects – a piano, a doll,
a cello, a hat – each with its own separate existence.
In this dynamic, moving portrait, Wright represents his
mother's shrinking world, a collection of disconnected
memories symbolised by the objects from her past.

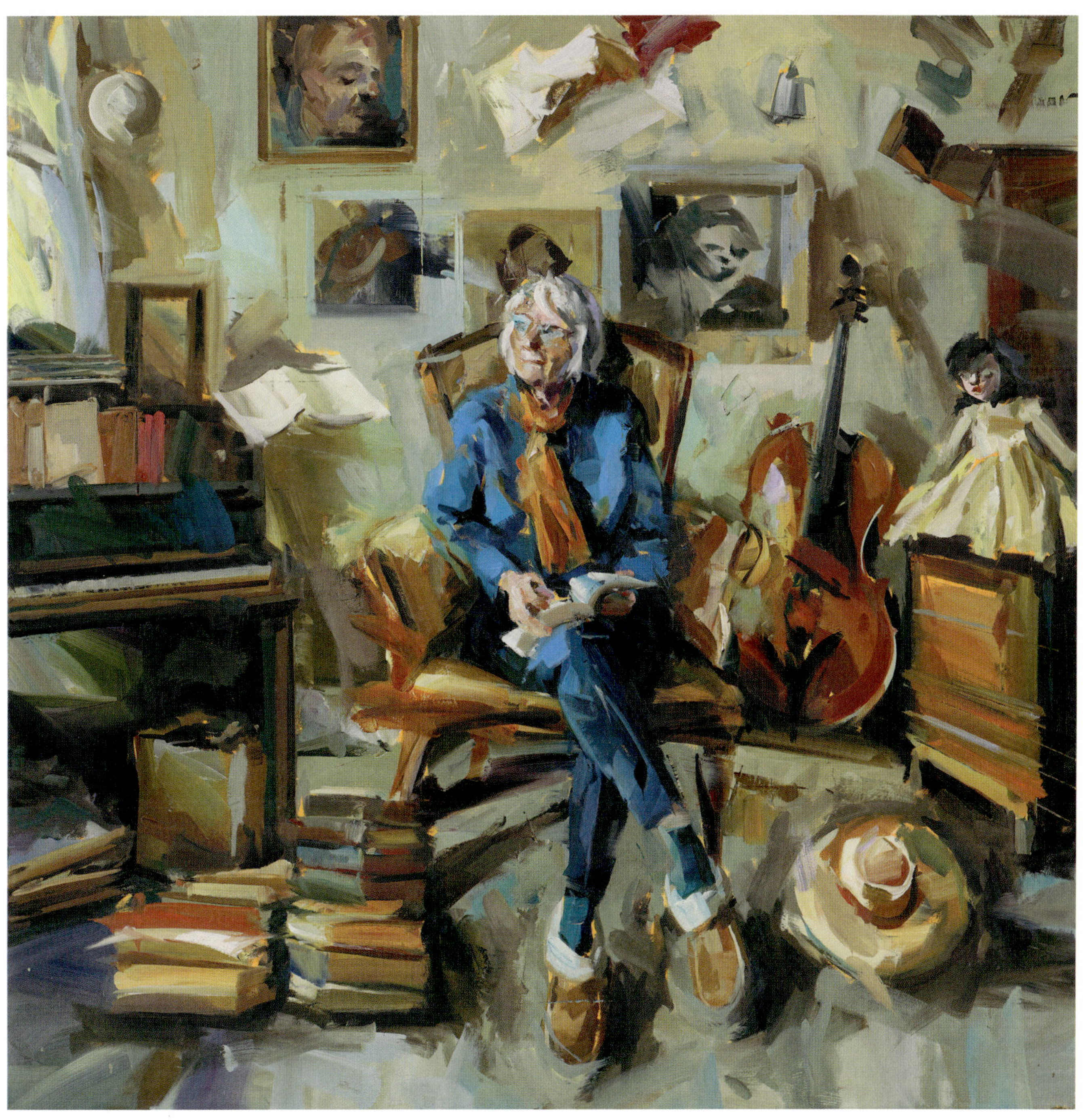

Archie Franks
Self-Portrait in my Andy Warhol Skull T-shirt, 2024
Oil on canvas
760 × 610mm

The thickly applied paint combines with the intense contrast between the clothing and background to provide a compelling formal compositional structure for this self-portrait. Inspired by Frans Hals's *Young Man holding a Skull (Vanitas)* (1626–8), the artist creates a contemporary instance of the traditional iconography of *memento mori*: a reminder of the audience's mortality; the Andy Warhol t-shirt continuing the artist's fascination with pop culture and the gothic.

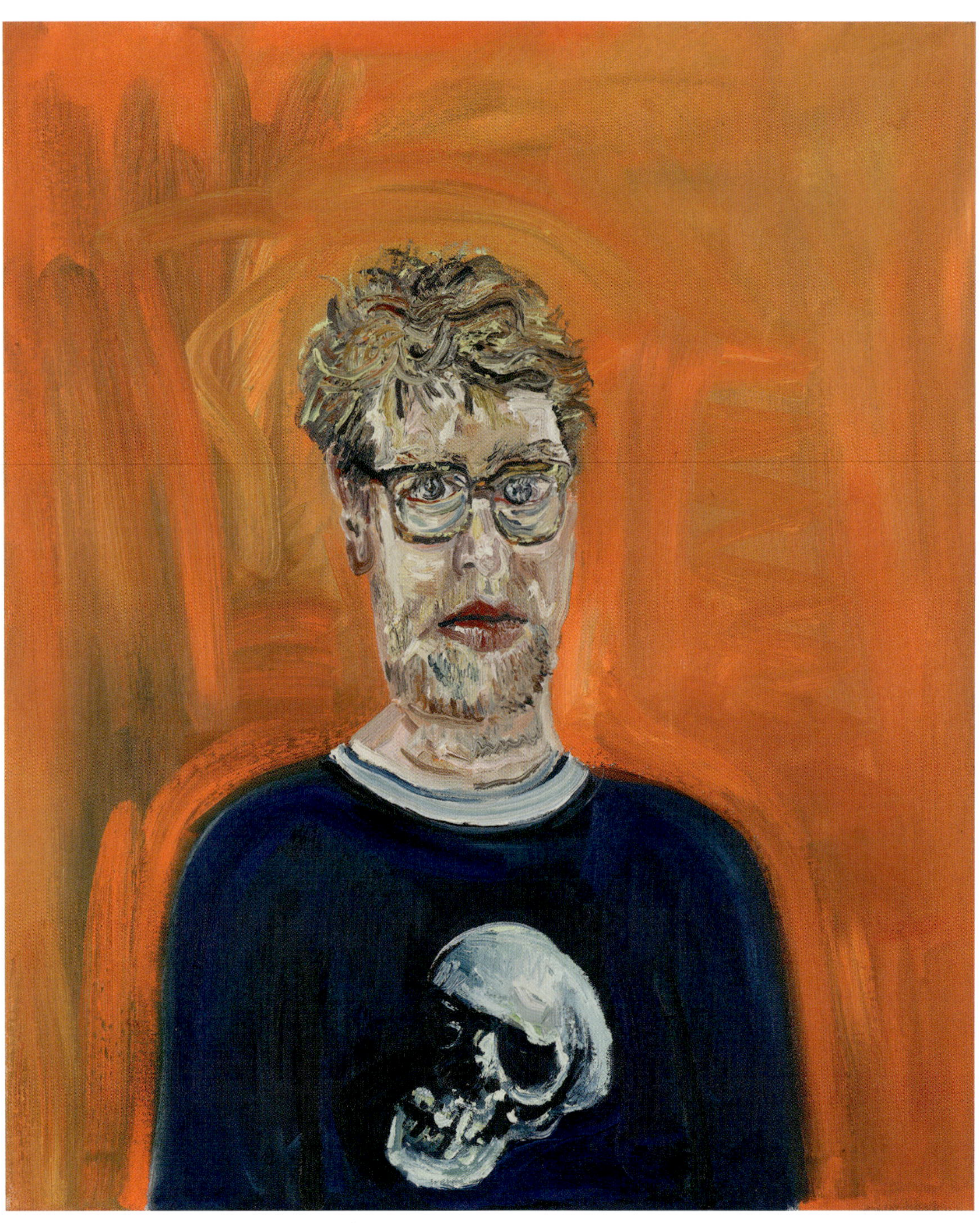

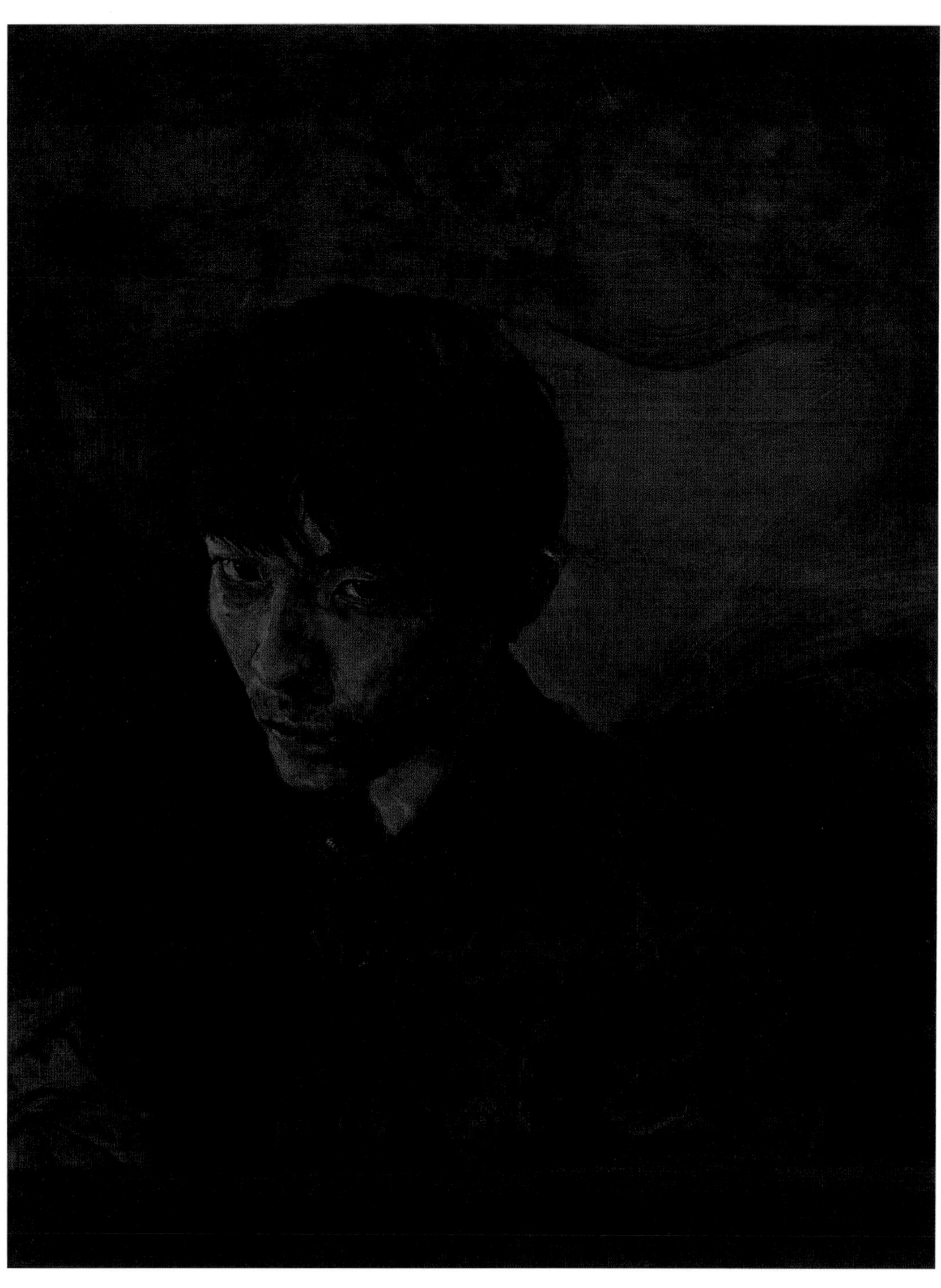

Li Ning
Portrait of K, 2024
Oil on canvas
800 × 600mm

Brooding, and conveying a strong sense of intimacy with the sitter, Li Ning casts his friend in a deep shadow that contrasts with the light, drawing the viewer into the sitters penetrating gaze. Completed in 2024, *Portrait of K* is the product of many minor adjustments over its seven years of creation. The portrait was made from a combination of sittings from life, photographic studies and memory.

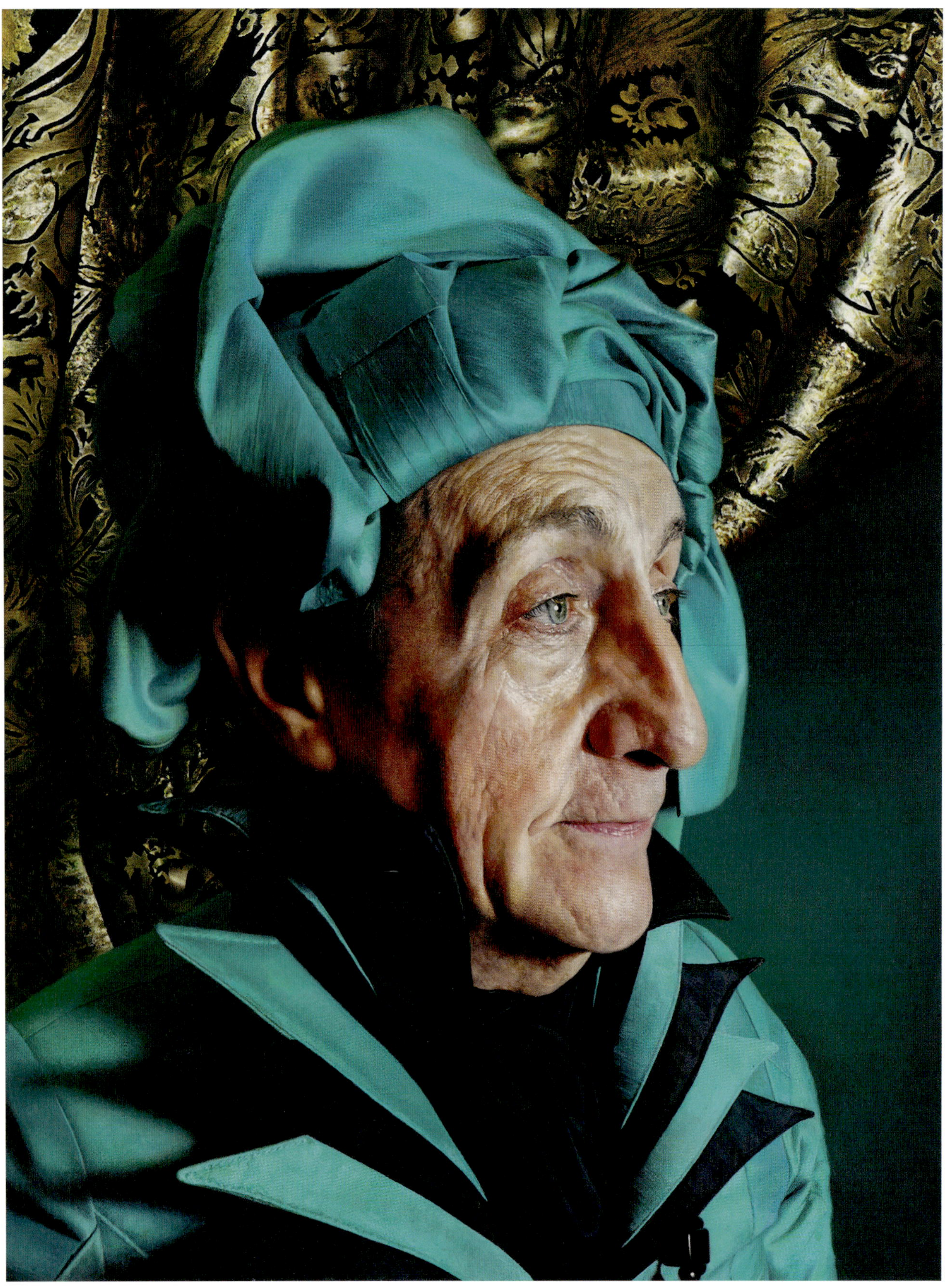

Simon Thomas Braiden
Philip Sallon, 2025
Oil on board
440 × 320mm

Philip Sallon is an impresario and sub-cultural pioneer, and was prominent in the Punk and New Romantic movements of the 1970s and 1980s. Simon Thomas Braiden seeks to depict Sallon's flamboyance through style and colour. The rendered textures of the skin and textiles imbue this painting with a powerful tactile quality; while the composition, subject matter and detailed techniques reference Jan van Eyck's *Portrait of a Man (Self-Portrait?)* (1433).

Ant Carver
Old Friends or Familiar Faces, 2025
Oil on linen
1000 × 800mm

Old Friends or Familiar Faces explores the metaphor of
the black dog and its contradictory symbolism: from a
reference to bad omens or depression to a representation
of belonging or guardianship. The sitter first modelled
for Ant Carver in 2020, and has since 'been a model that
I've returned to repeatedly as my work has evolved.' This
portrait is based on a series of quick charcoal sketches,
small painted studies, and experiments with composition
and colour.

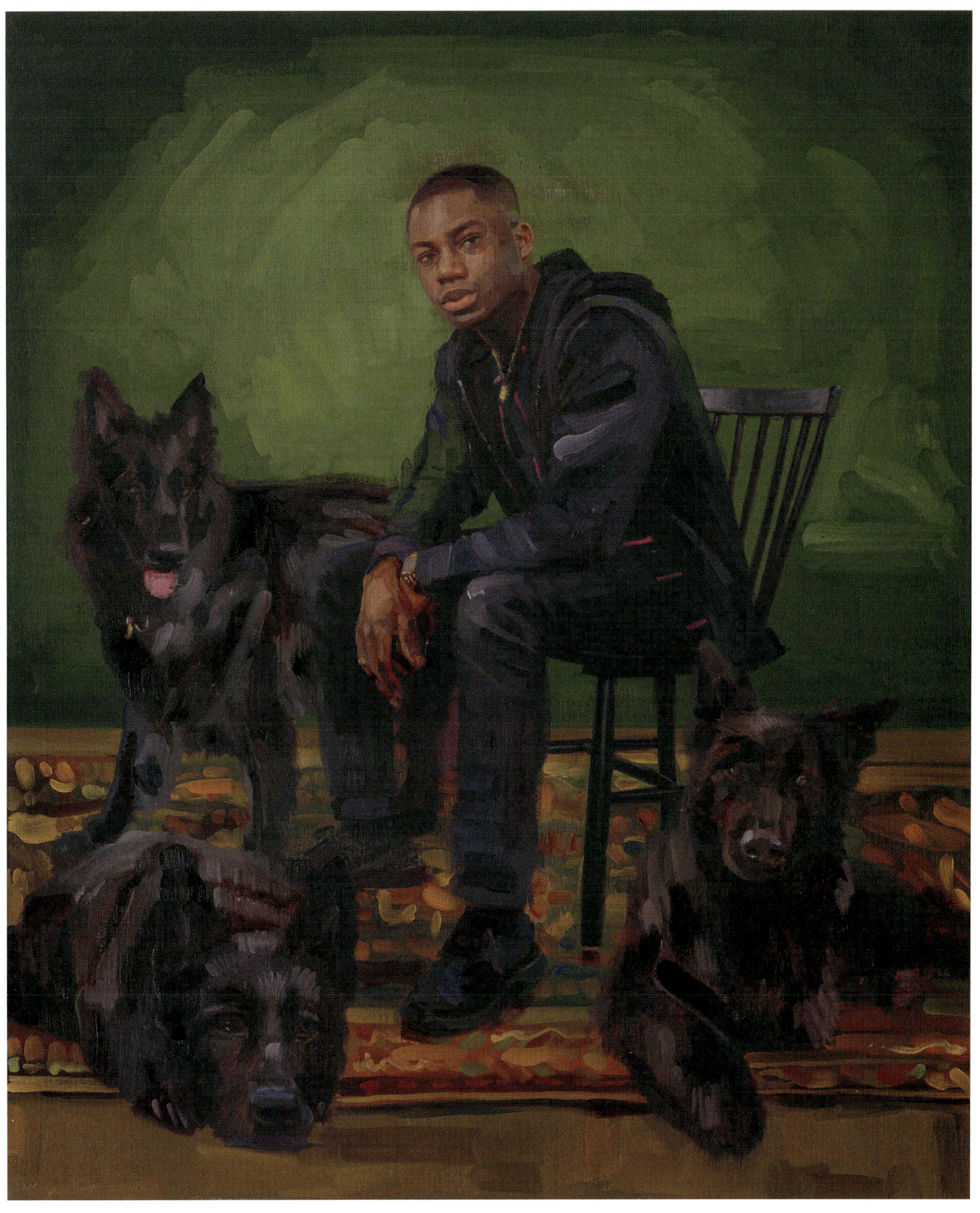

Thomas Arthurton
After the Concert, 2025
Oil and charcoal on canvas
1700 × 1050mm

Thomas Arthurton's *After the Concert* was inspired by
his love of classical music and represents Jacob Meining,
violinist and leader of the Bruckner Orchestra in Linz,
Austria. Seated and viewed from above, against a briefly
sketched charcoal interior, the sitter adopts a complex
pose embodying post-performance exhaustion. The
work is filled with a sense of uncertainty, fragility and
ambiguity, while the disjunction between his formal
attire and pink trainers expresses both tradition and
contemporaneity.

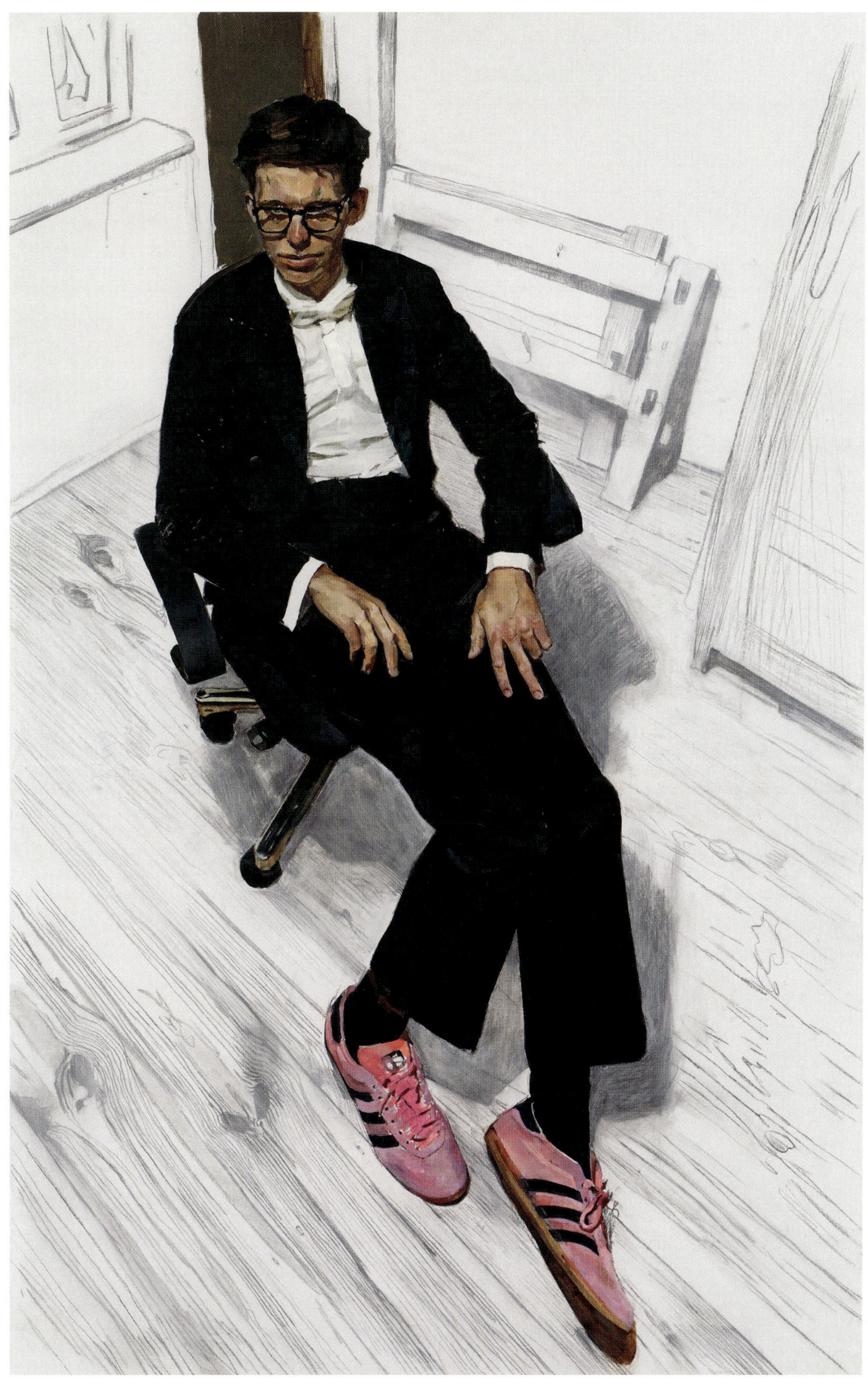

Emily Stainer
Mikayla, 2025
Oil on board
250 × 200mm

Emily Stainer captures a youthful image of pose and play. With the soft colours in the floral crown, rich skin tones and flowing lines of the neck and face, this beautifully painted profile portrait represents Mikayla, a friend of the artist's daughter. Mikayla and Stainer's daughter share roots in Southern Africa, have lived in several different countries and are now based in Brisbane, Australia. Influenced by Elizabethan miniature painting, the artist explores portraiture's connections to belonging through the sitter's identity.

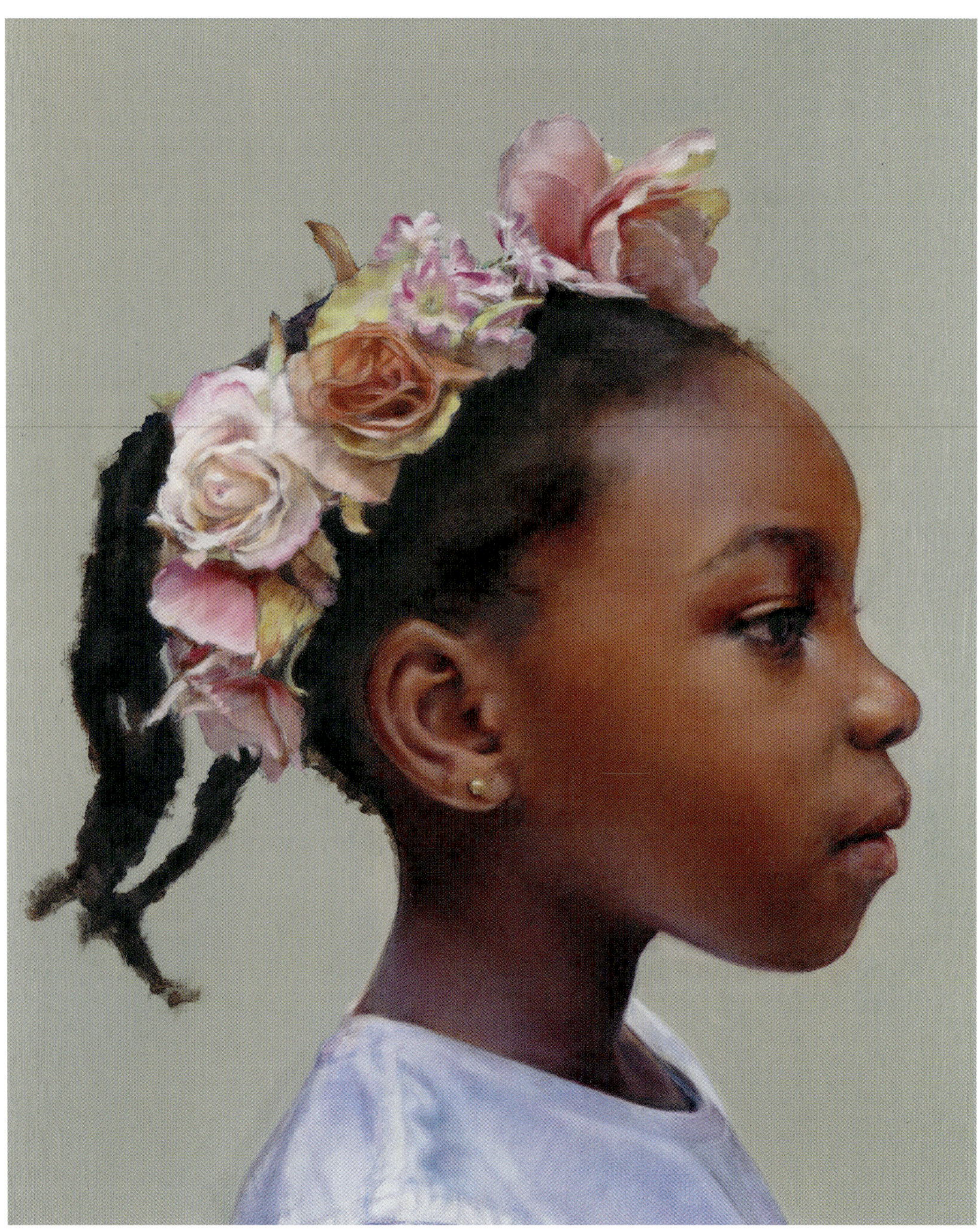

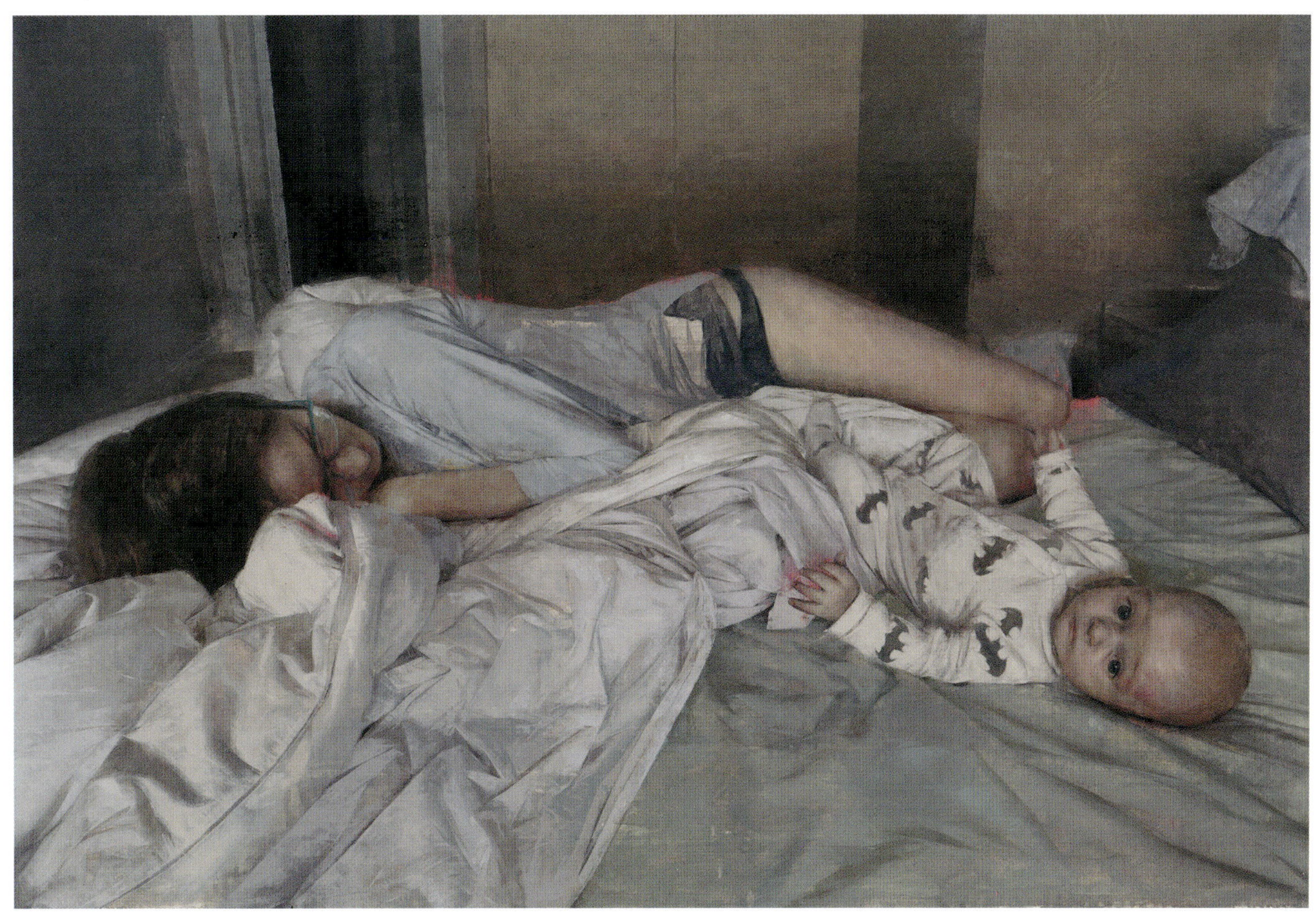

Diego José Aznar Remón
Mother, 2024
Oil on board
700 × 1000mm

Composed in muted tones, with momentary flashes of pink, this portrait by Spanish artist Diego José Aznar Remón represents his wife and son. The artist recalls that he came across this familiar domestic scene, noticing his exhausted wife enveloped in the folds of the sheet, while also contemplating the psychology in his son's wide-eyed, unknowing stare. The portrait reveals the process of production in the ruled lines covering the child's face.

Lucille Dweck
Ollie and Orlando (The New York Couple), 2024
Oil on linen
2000 × 800mm

The symmetry and contrast of this carefully composed
portrait expresses the nature of the relationship represented.
Lucille Dweck's *Ollie and Orlando (The New York Couple)*
pictures her two friends hand in hand, staring deeply into
each other's eyes. The couple are dressed in blues and
blacks, visually striking against the red wall. Inspired by
the couples' love, Dweck 'had a very strong compulsion
to make this painting'. She seeks to express a message
of unity in a time of social and political division.

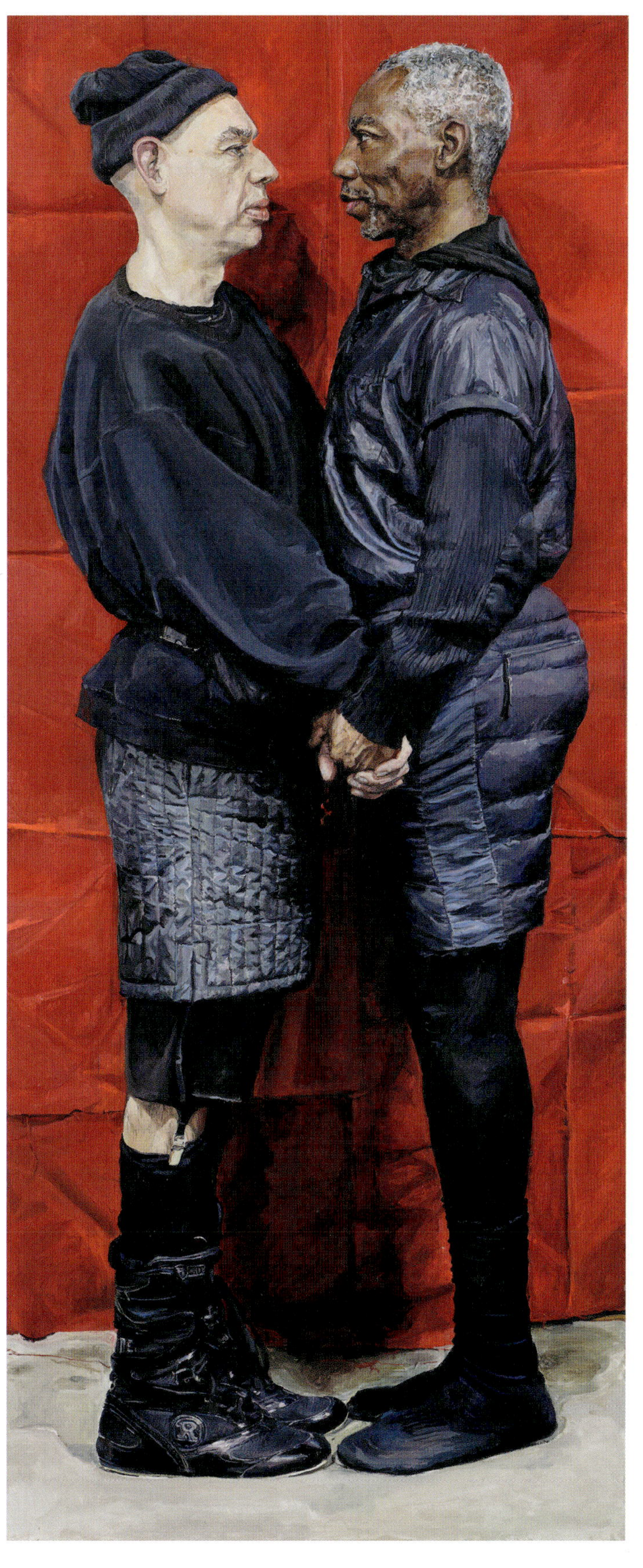

Comhghall Casey
Self-Portrait, 2024
Oil on canvas
300 × 270mm

This self-portrait presents a jarring perception of physical proximity to the sitter, and exhibits a pronounced tactility within each texture – the weave of the hat, the hairs of the beard and the skin under the eyes. This painting by, the Irish artist Comhghall Casey, is part of an ongoing series that aims to record the physical and mental process of aging while also documenting his changing technique and style. Created over a period of months, Casey uses a mirror and direct observation to capture his portrait from life.

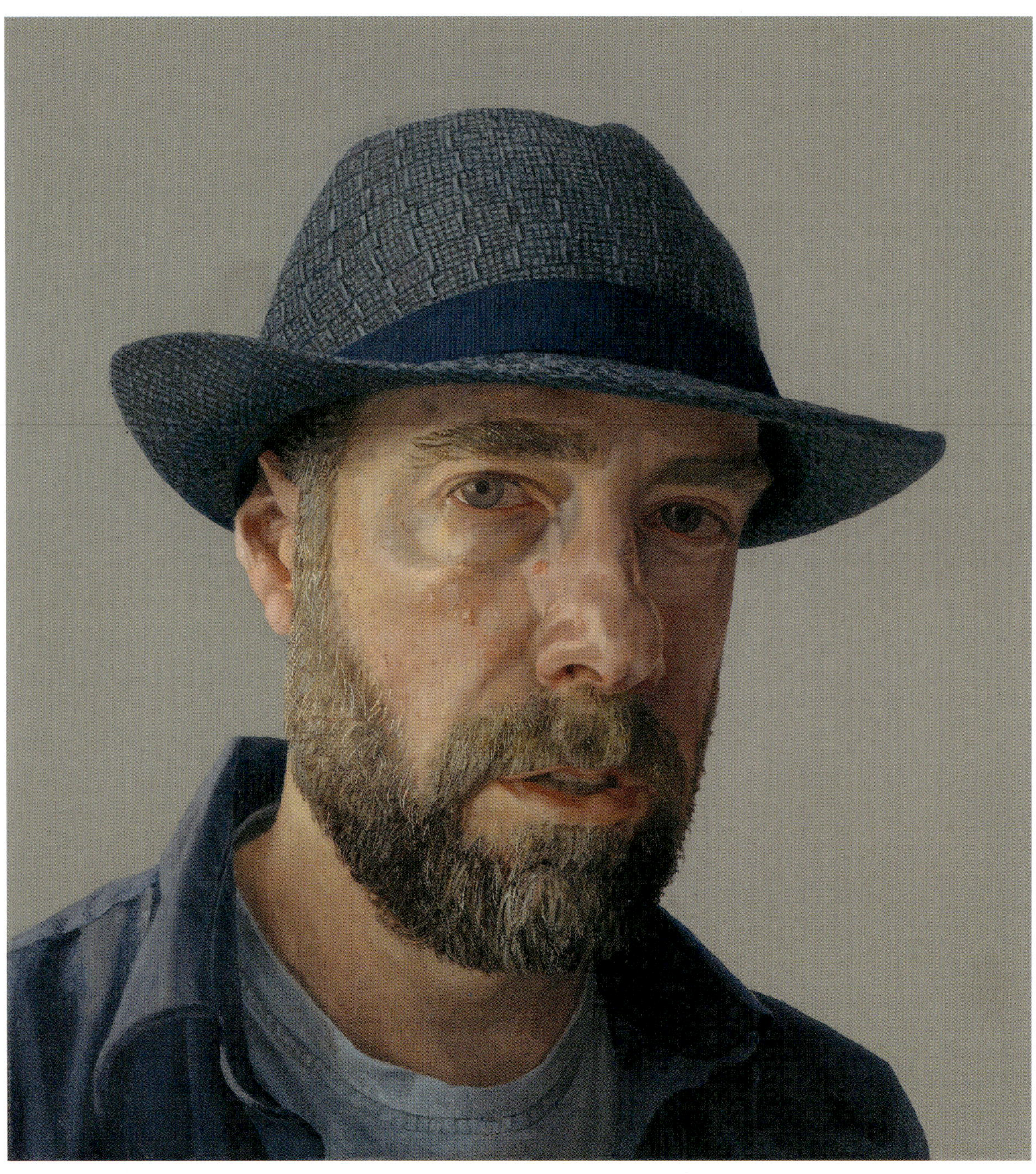

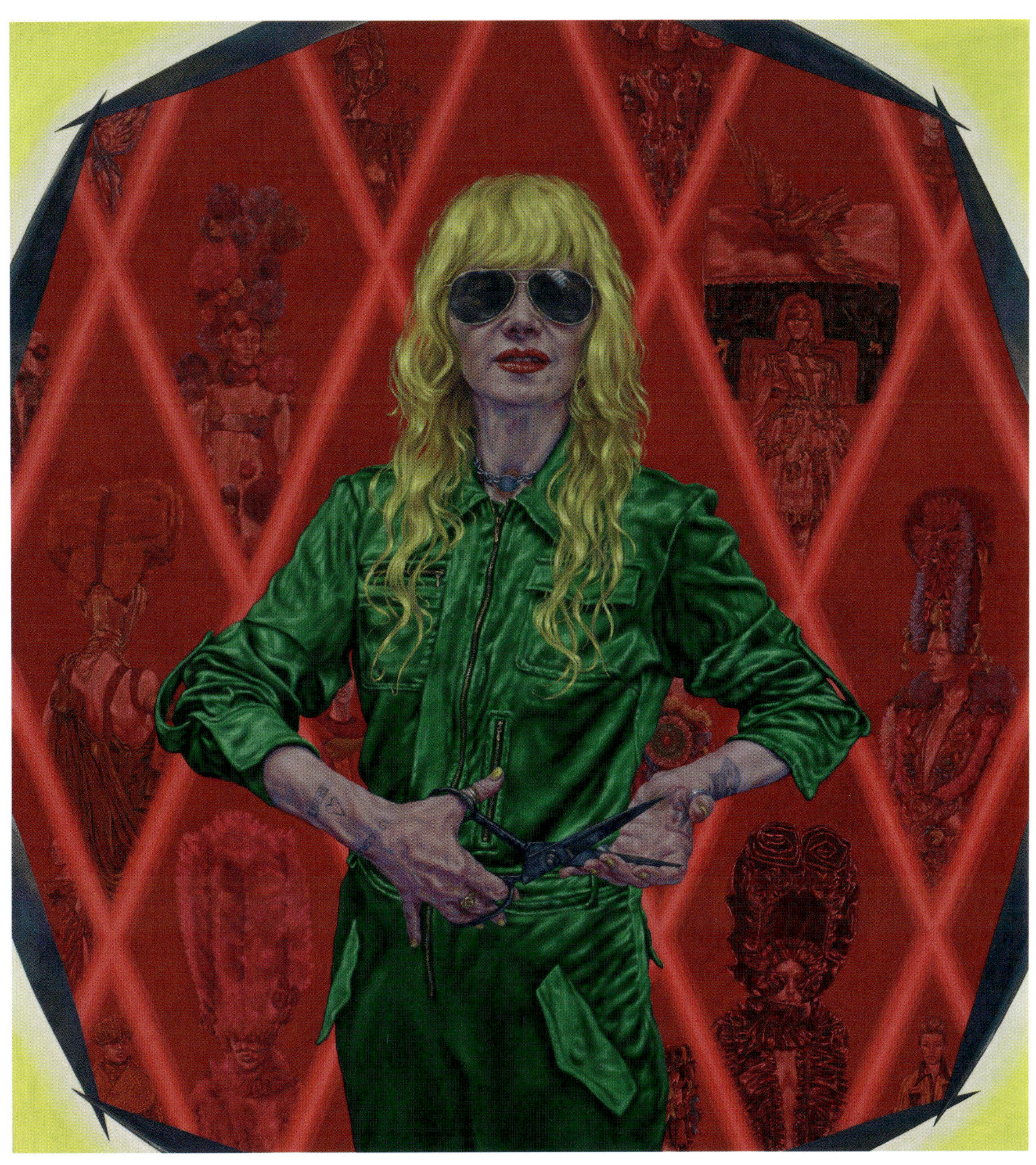

Roxana Halls
DR PAM HOGG, 2025
Oil on linen
1400 × 1200mm

Scottish fashion designer Pam Hogg collaborated with Roxana Halls when devising the pose for this arresting portrait. Dramatically displaying her favourite scissors, Hogg is dressed in a striking green jumpsuit set-off against a vivid red background with depictions of her designs. The artist aims to capture the sitter's 'fearless, inventive, and provocative' style and express her admiration for 'someone who is still at the forefront of avant-garde fashion in Britain and is still so vitally disruptive, unconventional and productive'.

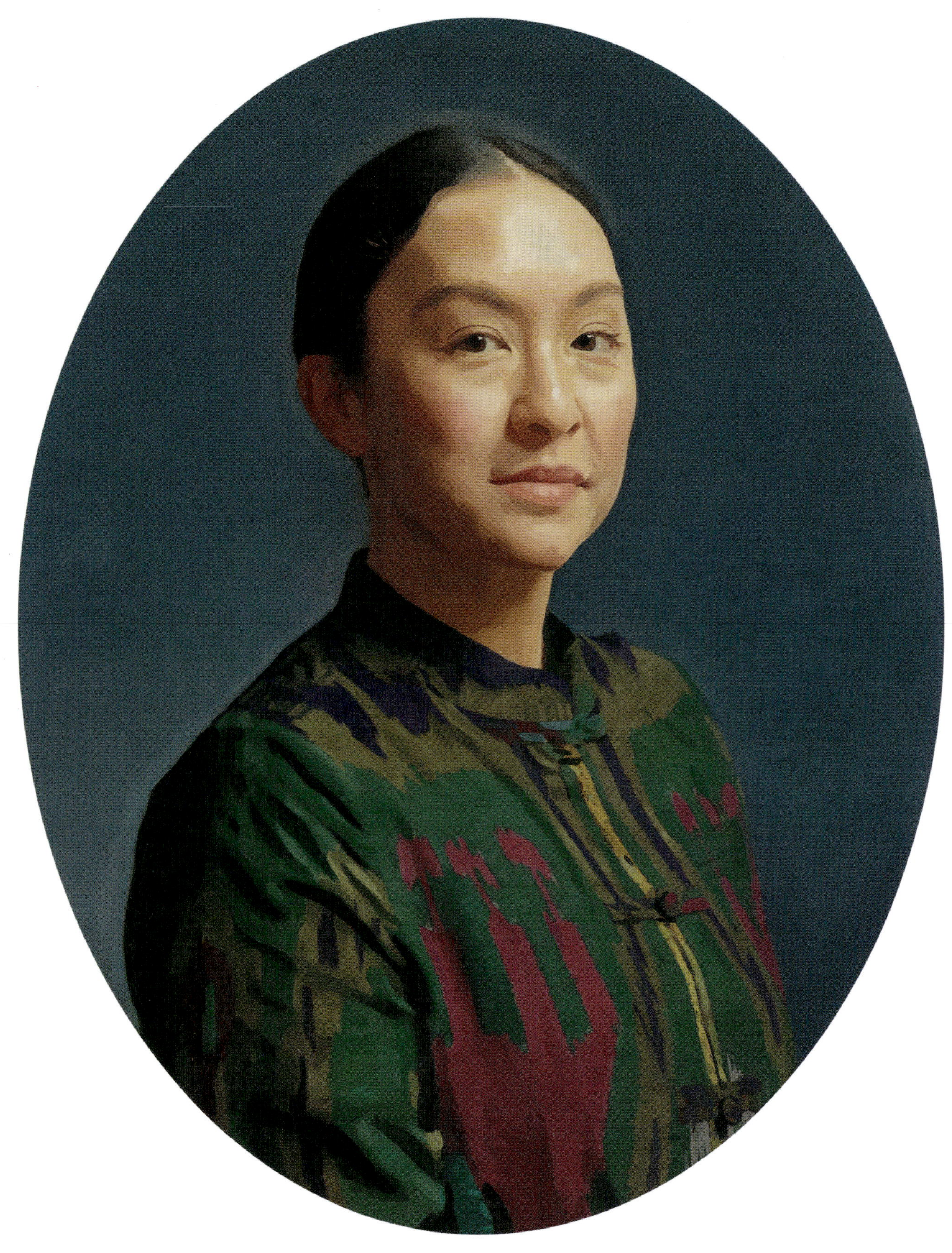

Jamie Routley
Elle, 2024
Oil on linen
650 × 450mm

An Old Master sense of quality and composition characterises Jamie Routley's oval portrait of Elle. A blend of the classical and modern is echoed through the sitter's contemporary, Asian-inspired silk ikat dress; while Elle's low bun hairstyle draws 'a quiet yet significant connection between Elle and her late paternal Korean grandmother, who used to wear her hair the same way.' This is symbolic of the sitter's pride in their Asian heritage. Quiet and understated, but exuding a calm confidence, this refined painting might give access to the personality of the sitter.

Pippa Hale-Lynch
The Echo – Self-Portrait, 2024
Oil on panel
306 × 230mm

Pippa Hale-Lynch's self-portrait has the quality of a
doubly exposed photograph, or one that has slipped
and smudged in the process of development. The artist
presents a distorted and ghostly image, expressing a fluid
and dynamic artistic identity. Akin to much of Hale-Lynch's
work, this painting explores themes of solitude and grief
stemming from the loss of her mother. The rendering of
movement and visual obscurity reflects 'the ephemerality
of the human experience'.

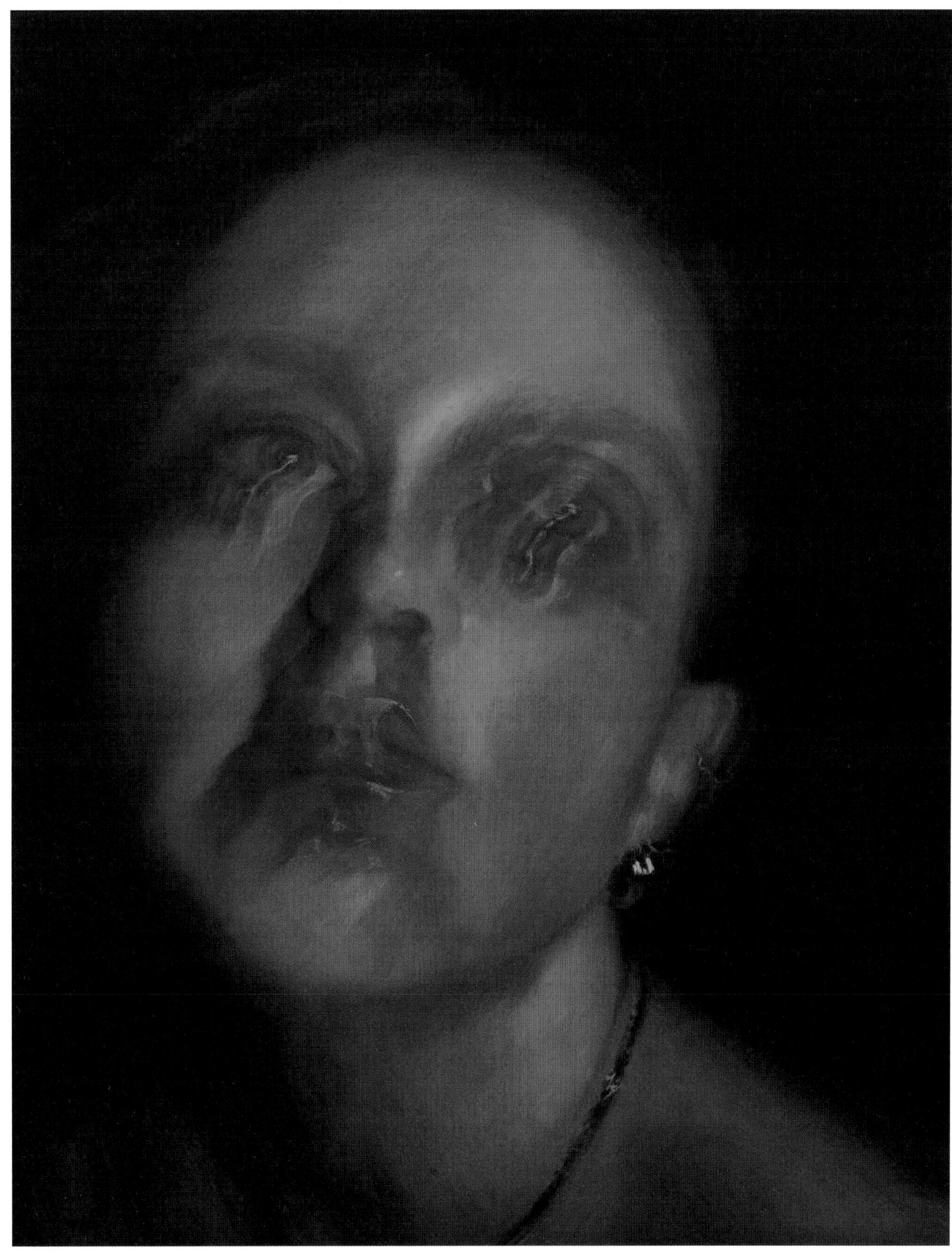

Nathalie Beauvillain Scott
Maxine – Business Woman Wife Mother Nurse, 2024
Oil on canvas
500 × 500mm

Nathalie Beauvillain Scott's striking, hyperrealist portrait
of Maxine, nurse and businesswoman, creates a sense
of direct connection between the subject and viewer.
One in a series of portraits entitled *Faces of Guildford*,
the work was originally conceived in recognition of
Maxine's many achievements, but as the sittings went
on 'I realised I really wanted the viewer to be able to
perceive her strength, compassion and caring personality.'

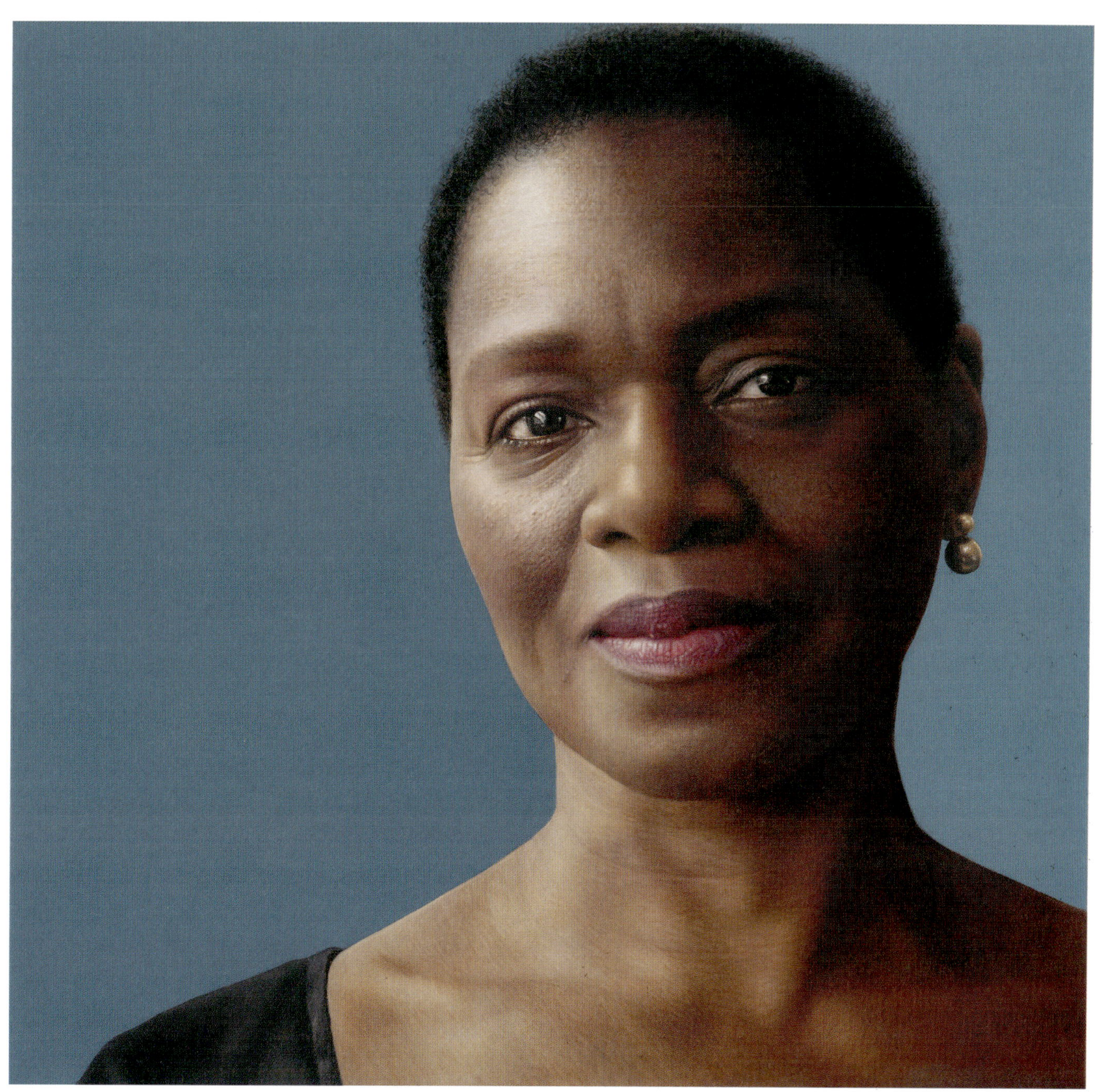

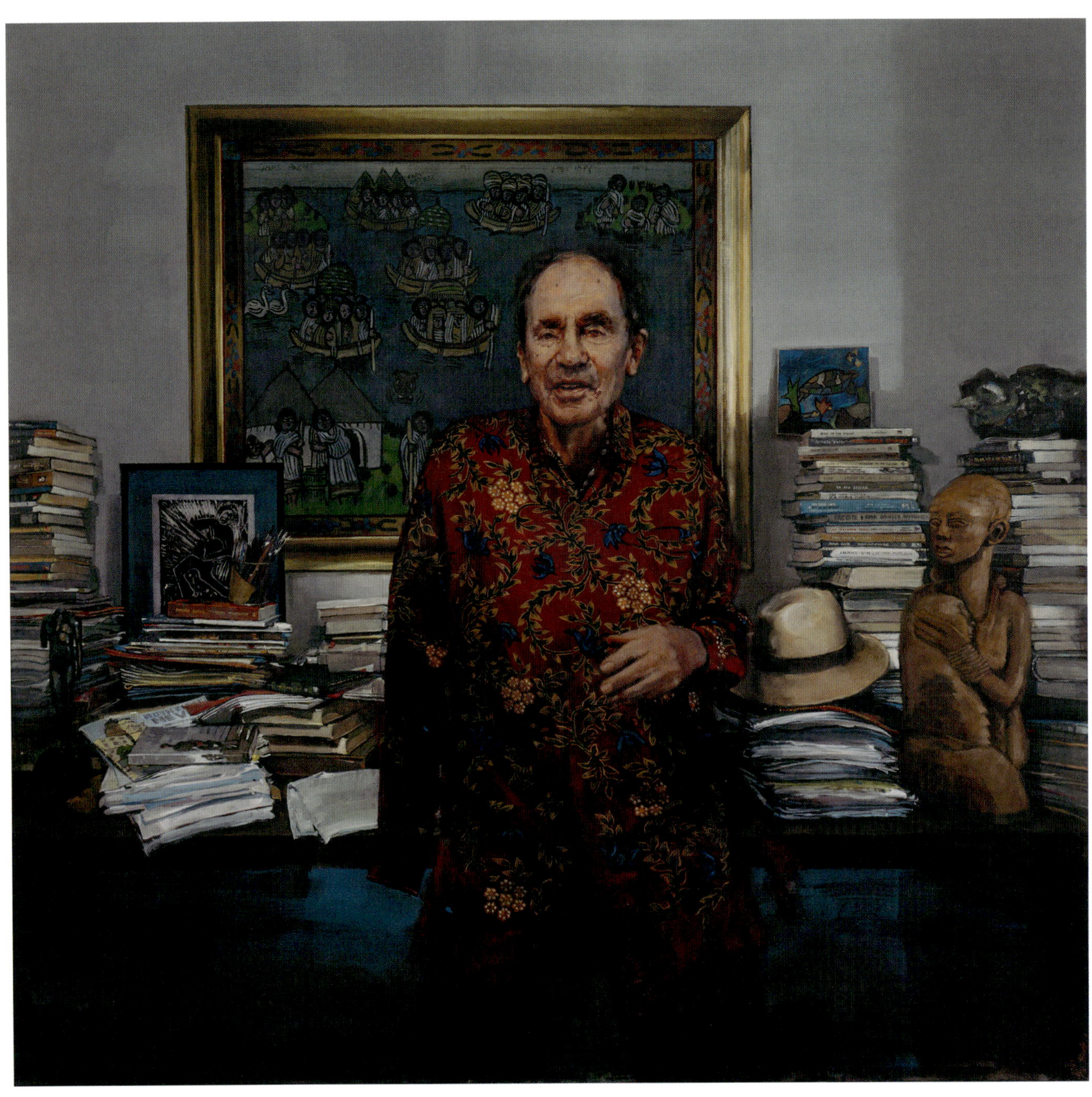

Ashley Oglivy
Call me Albie, 2024
Oil on aluminium
1150 × 1150mm

In 1988, South African lawyer and anti-apartheid activist, Albie Sachs survived a car bomb assassination attempt, losing his right arm and the vision in his left eye. Sachs went on to help draft a new constitution for South Africa and was appointed a Constitutional Court Judge by Nelson Mandela, following the country's first democratic elections. Ashley Ogilvy's portrait depicts a flamboyantly dressed Sachs standing before piles of books and among some works from his own art collection.

Brenda Zlamany
*Two Dogs (Portrait of David Hockney
Inspired by Whistler's Mother)*, 2024
Oil on linen
1524 × 1524mm

Brenda Zlamany represents one of the most celebrated British contemporary artists, David Hockney. Having known Hockney since she sat for him in the 1990s, this painting recalls a recent visit to his studio, capturing a moment of 'quiet joy'. The title and composition reference the 1871 painting *Whistler's Mother* by James McNeill Whistler. With Hockney's *Two Dogs* (1998) on the wall, printed by the master printer Maurice Payne, and Zlamany's own self-portrait subtly reflected in the glass, the painting expresses ideas of community and shared history.

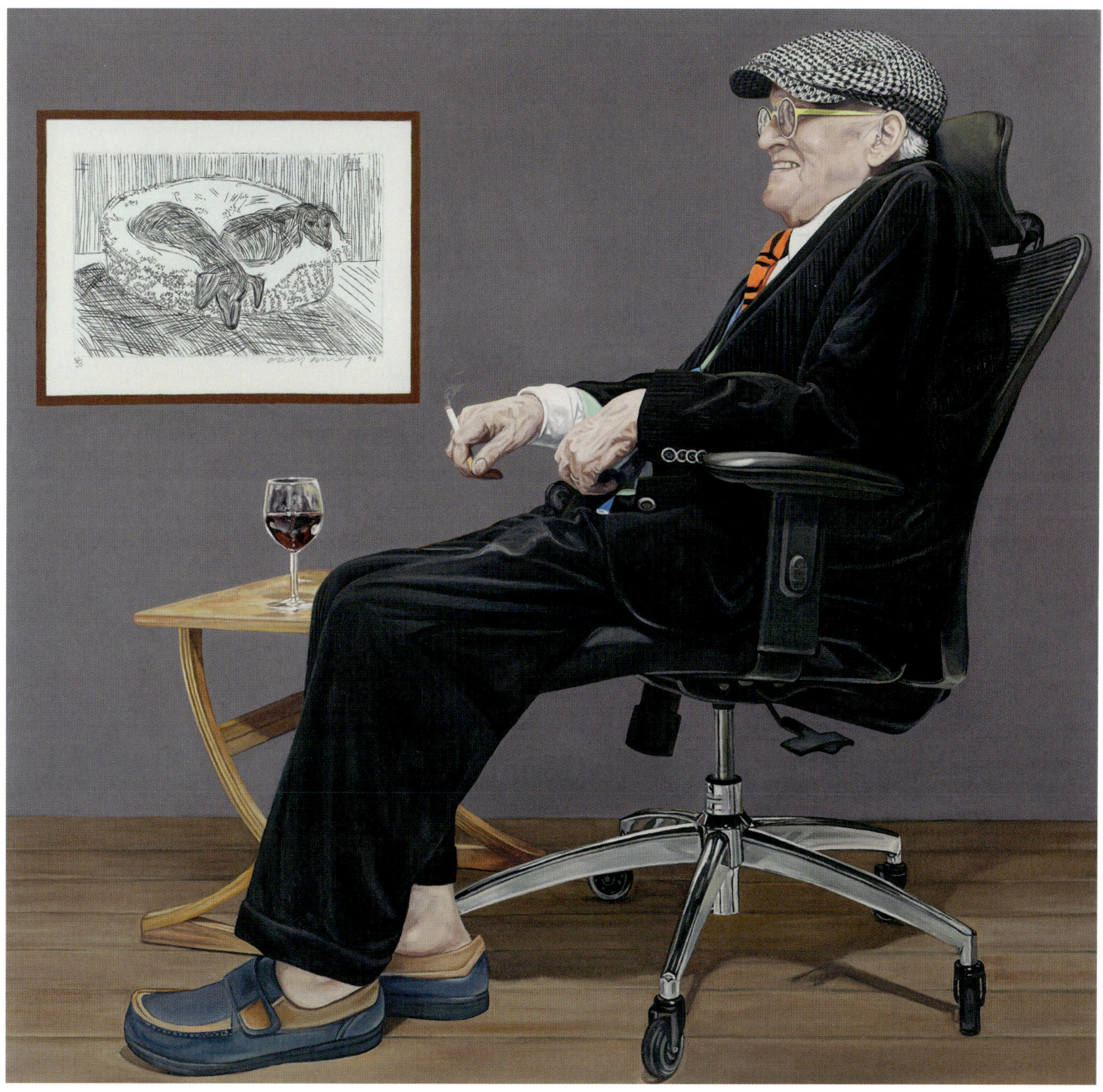

Rachit Khandelwal
The Sitter – Self-Portrait, 2024
Oil on canvas
710 × 610mm

A curious emerald green pervades every part of this unique self-portrait. Emerging from under the sitter's slightly unkempt hair, and obscuring our view of his wide staring eyes, the colour is inescapable. Currently a student at Glasgow School of Art, Indian artist Rachit Khandelwal has presented a version of himself both anxious and introspective, 'a state of mind that I often find myself in', he writes. The strength of colour works at odds with the quietness of Khandelwal's pose.

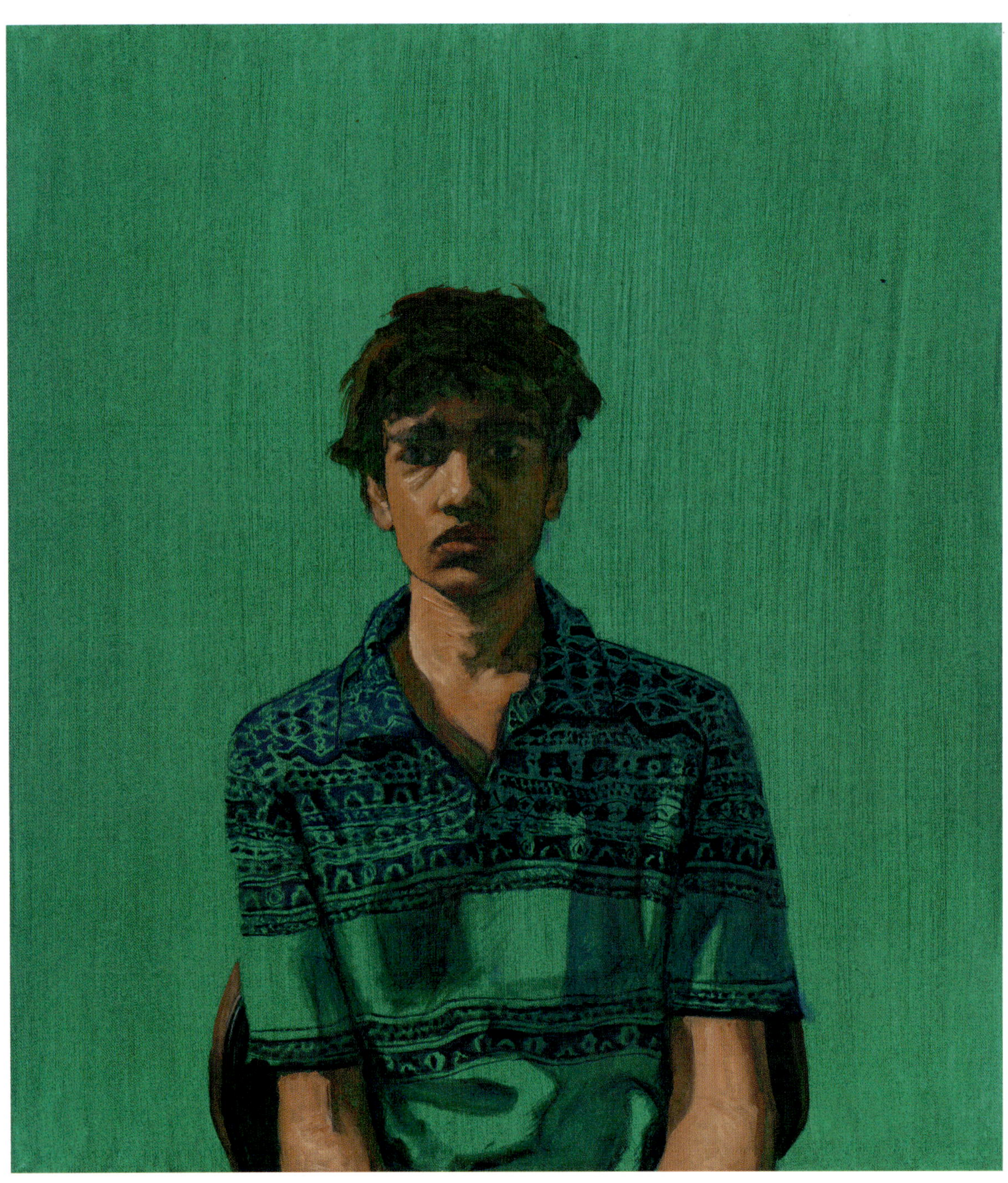

Finlay Trevor
Quest for The Mackintosh Man, 2024
Oil on board
800 × 600mm

While the country was in lockdown during the Covid pandemic, artist Finlay Trevor volunteered to help with the lambing on his local sheep farm in South Erradale in the Scottish Highlands. *Quest for The Mackintosh Man* is part of a larger body of work that documents life on the farm. Retired farmer, Willie Mackintosh, is depicted through woven brushwork of greys and browns in an expression of his thoughts on the land and the decline of the rural industry.

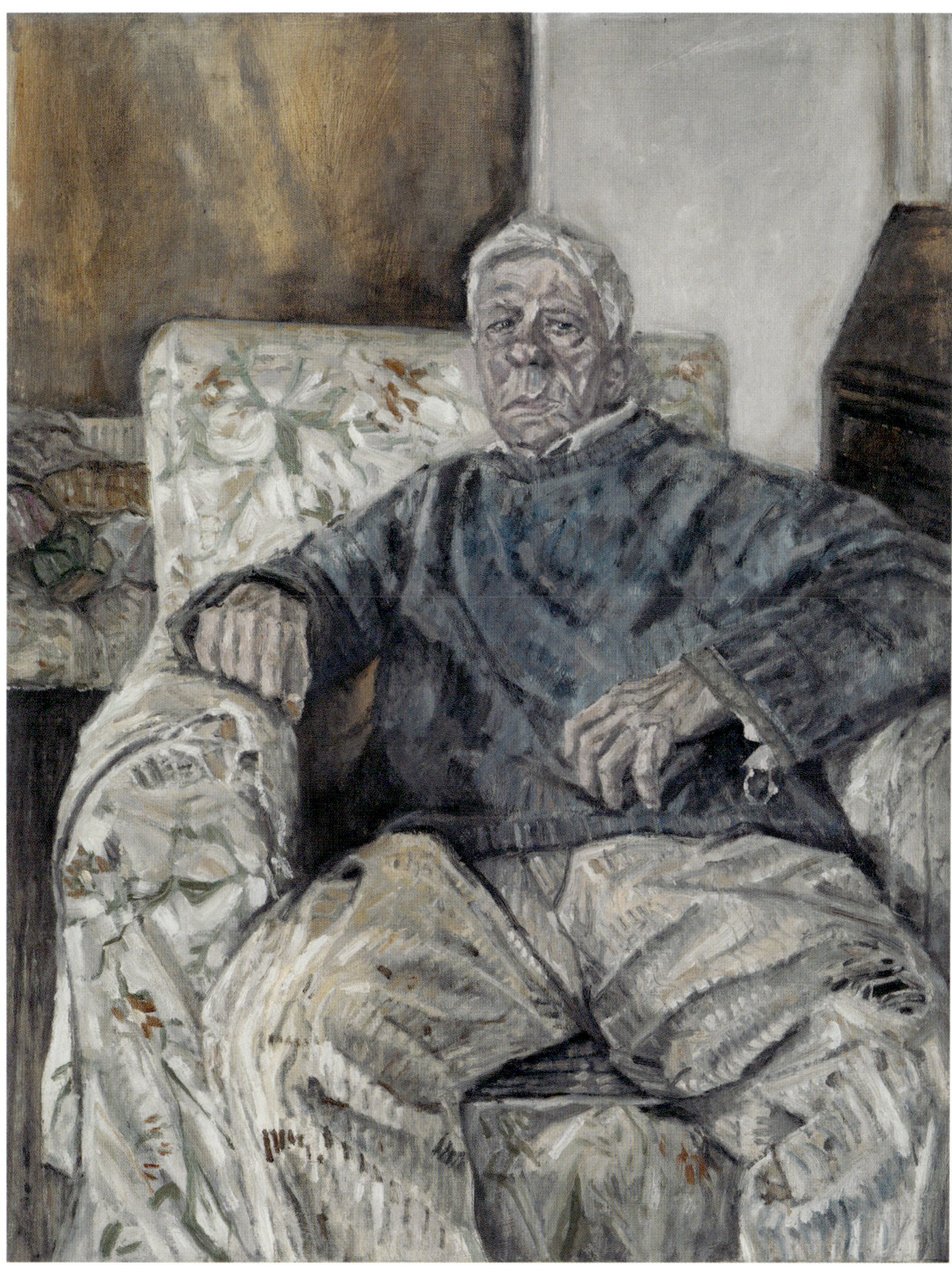

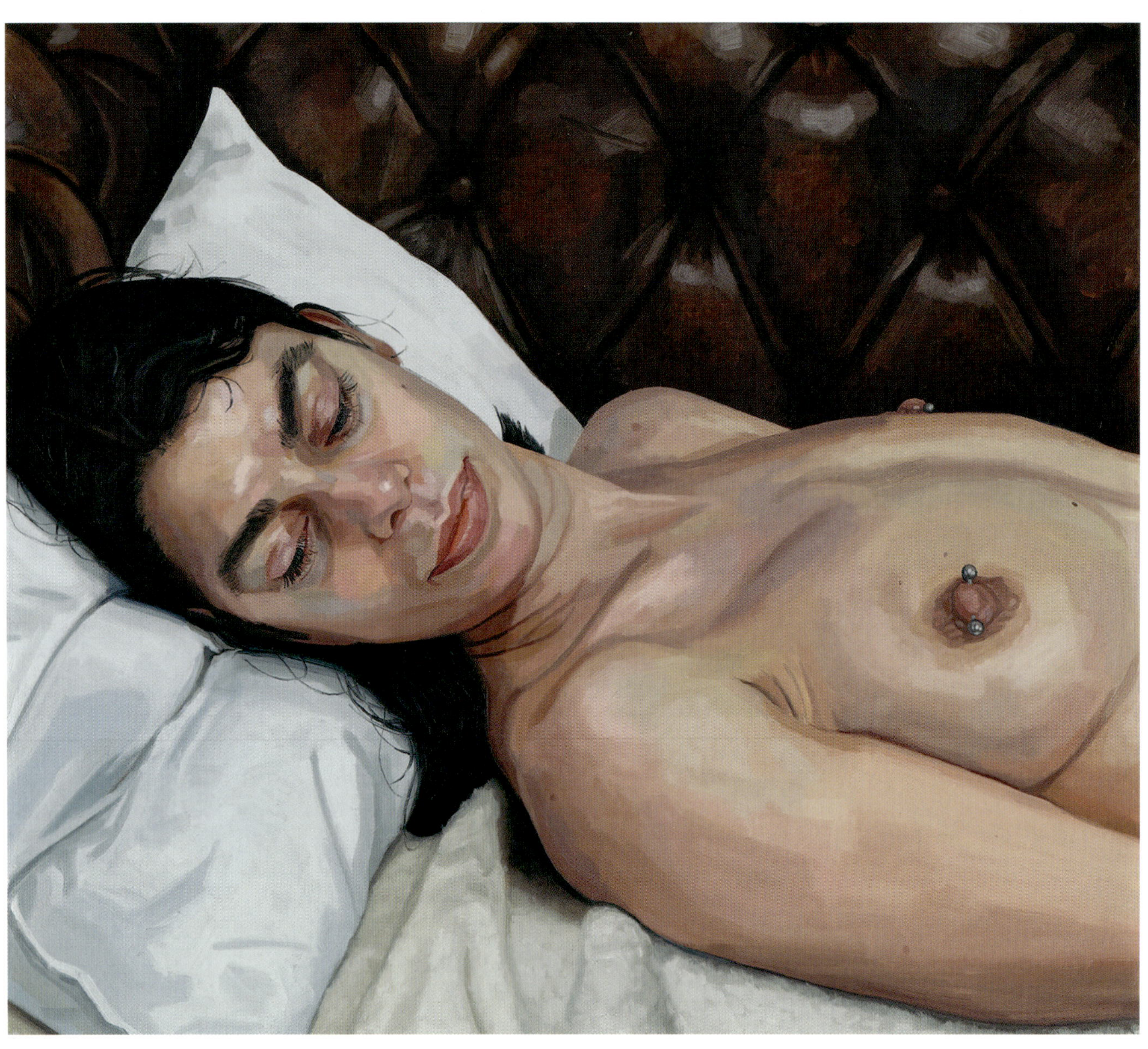

Richard Kitson
Alice IV, 2024
Oil on canvas
510 × 560mm

This is the fourth painting in a series of works focusing on Richard Kitson's model and friend, Alice. Both an exploration of the sitter and the process of portrait making itself, the artwork creates a feeling of authenticity. Composed as the sitter naturally arranged herself in the studio, a sense of intimacy is given by the close focus and cropping of the torso. Kitson produced this portrait over a period of months, allowing him to 'take in more information about my sitter as their moods differ during the various sittings.'

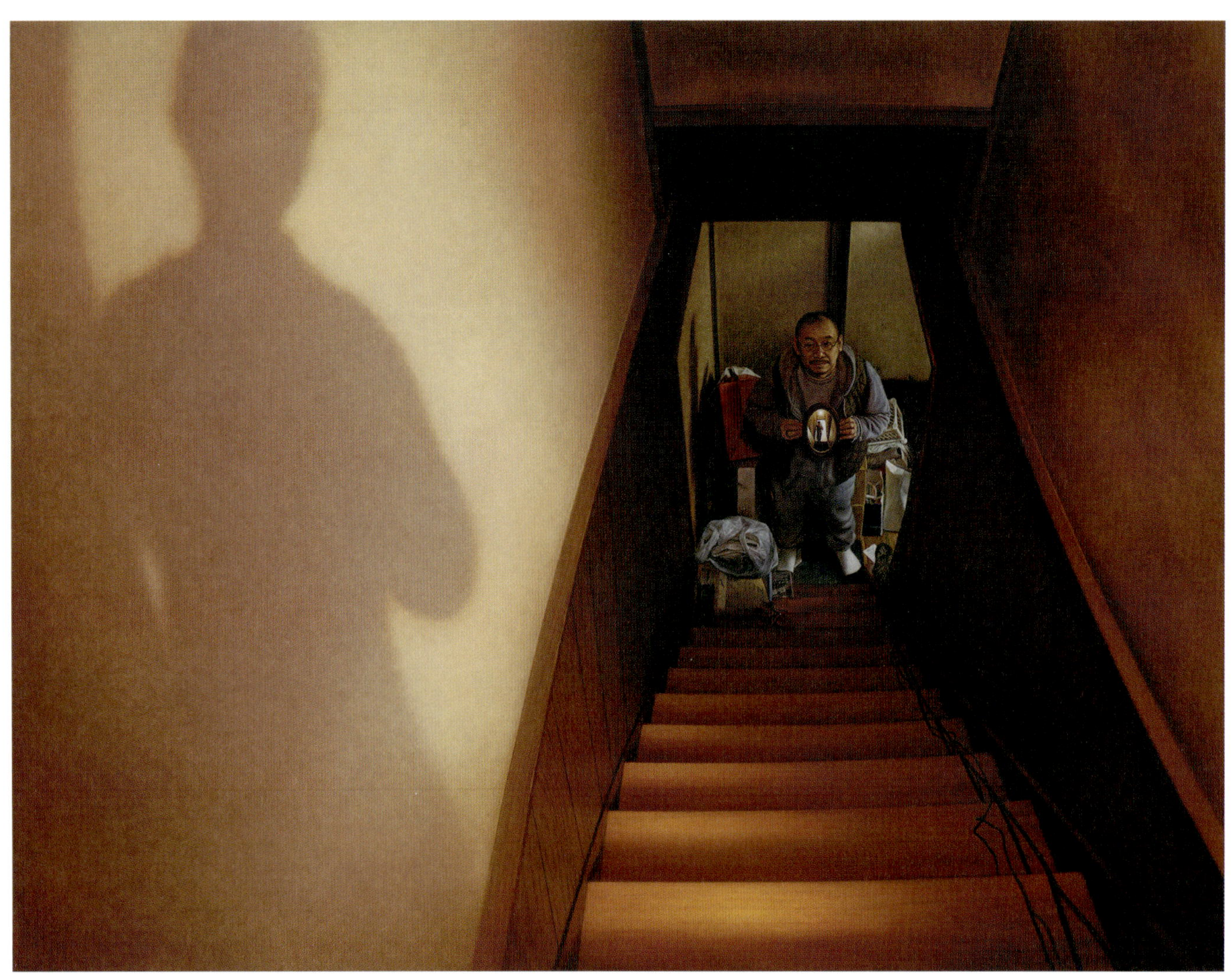

Shinji Ihara
Light and Shadow, 2025
Oil on canvas
727 × 910mm

In Japanese artist Shinji Ihara's portrait of his partner, the complex perspective places the viewer at the centre of a dizzying relay between artist and sitter. Inspired by Jan van Eyck's *The Arnolfini Portrait* (1434), and created with a similarly meticulous and highly sophisticated technique, the painting is part of a long art historical tradition of using mirrors to examine spatial and human relationships.

Simon Watkins
Claire, 2025
Oil on canvas
700 × 950mm

Simon Watkins's portrait depicts his wife's grandmother Claire, who lives with dementia. Seated at a table and listening to music with closed eyes, the minimalist quality of the painting captures the still, calm of an inner moment. The work highlights the peace that music can bring to those with dementia. Watkins's subtle and poetic portrait is a profound reflection on light, space and the process of aging.

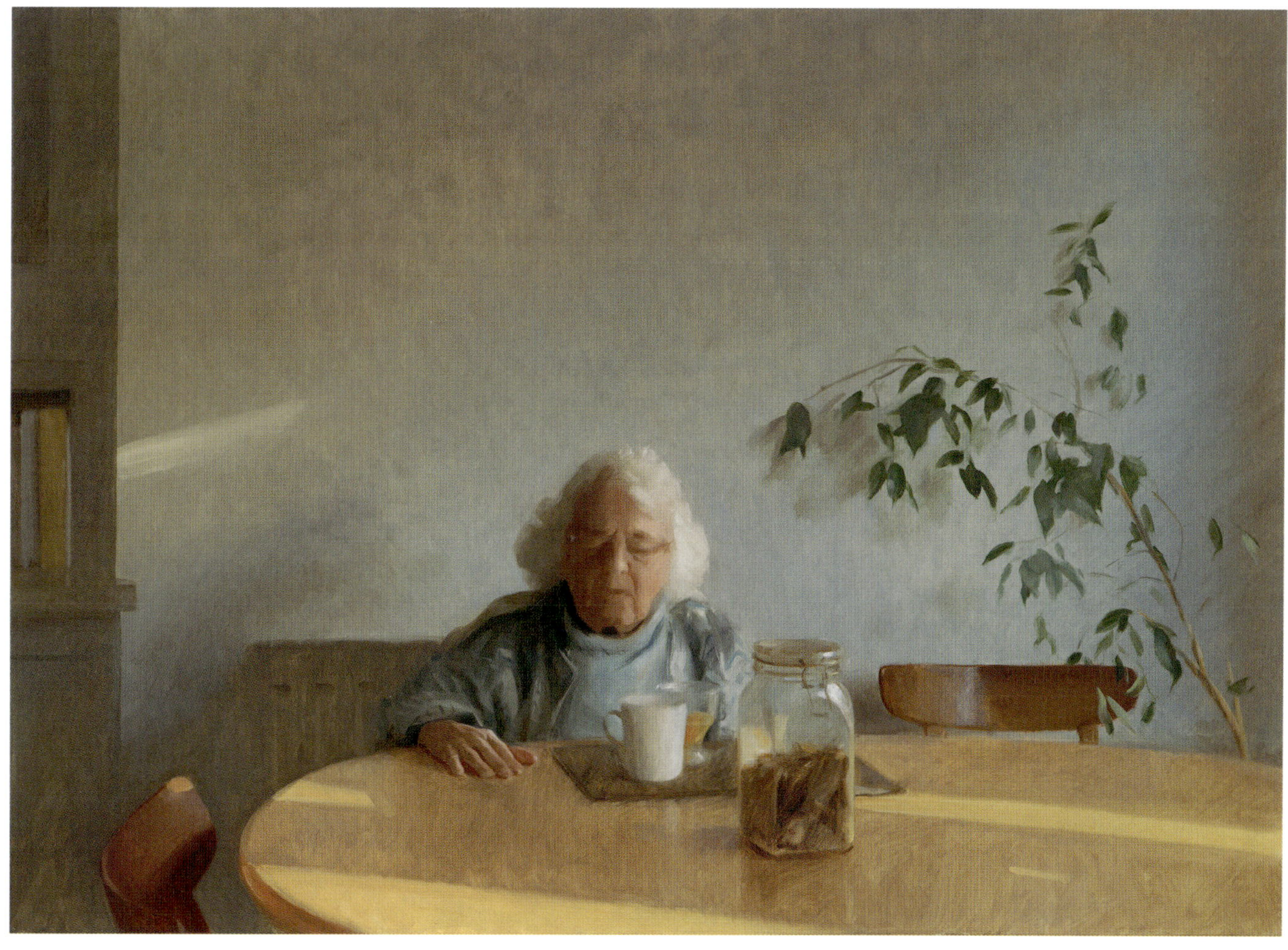

Xu Yang
Tangled Waves: Leda and the Swan
with Tang Dynasty Style Make-up, 2024
Oil on linen
2000 × 1700mm

This large, dramatic painting resists easy viewing through
the depth of the black tones and its sharp contrast with
the mask-like, porcelain face. Chinese artist Xu Yang
achieves such depth within her black paint through a mix
of traditional pigments, such as ultramarine and madder.
A product of cross-cultural influence, this recreation of
the Greek myth of 'Leda and the Swan' visually connects
the two protagonists through echoing the Tang Dynasty
court-style red lips of Leda and the beak of the black
swan. Using herself as a model, the artist aims to raise
important questions about diversity and gender.

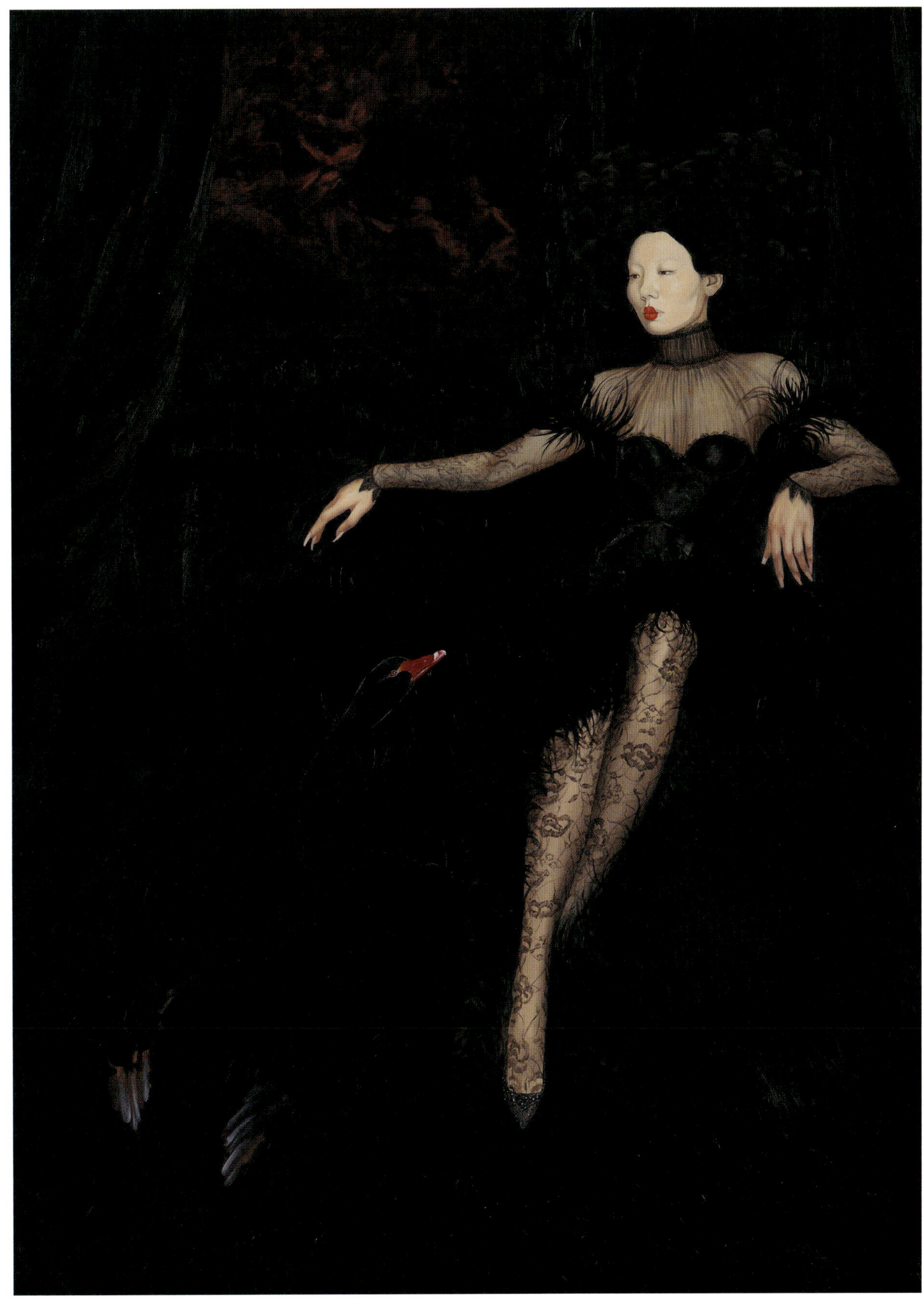

Nelson Hernandez
Ukranian Girl, 2025
Oil on board
760 × 610mm

A female figure with her back to the viewer stands at a
window, through which shines a wintry light illuminating
individual strands of her light blonde hair. Chilean artist
Nelson Hernandez's spectral portrait of his Ukranian
friend, Kseniia, captures a brief moment in time: 'I was
moved by her stillness as she gazed out the window.
Suddenly, the drawing in her hoodie evoked in me a scene
of war, a metaphor of her past and the burden she carries.'

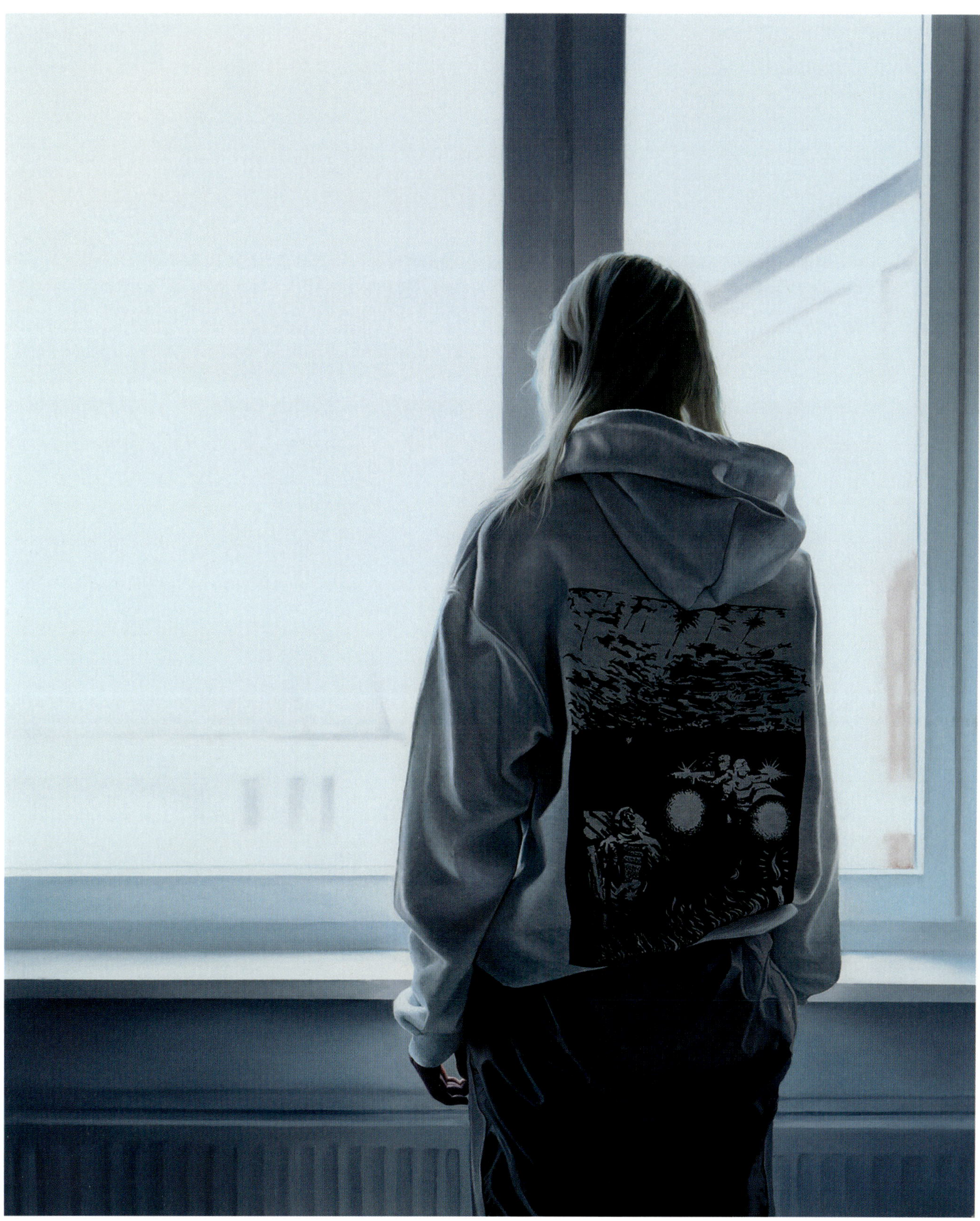

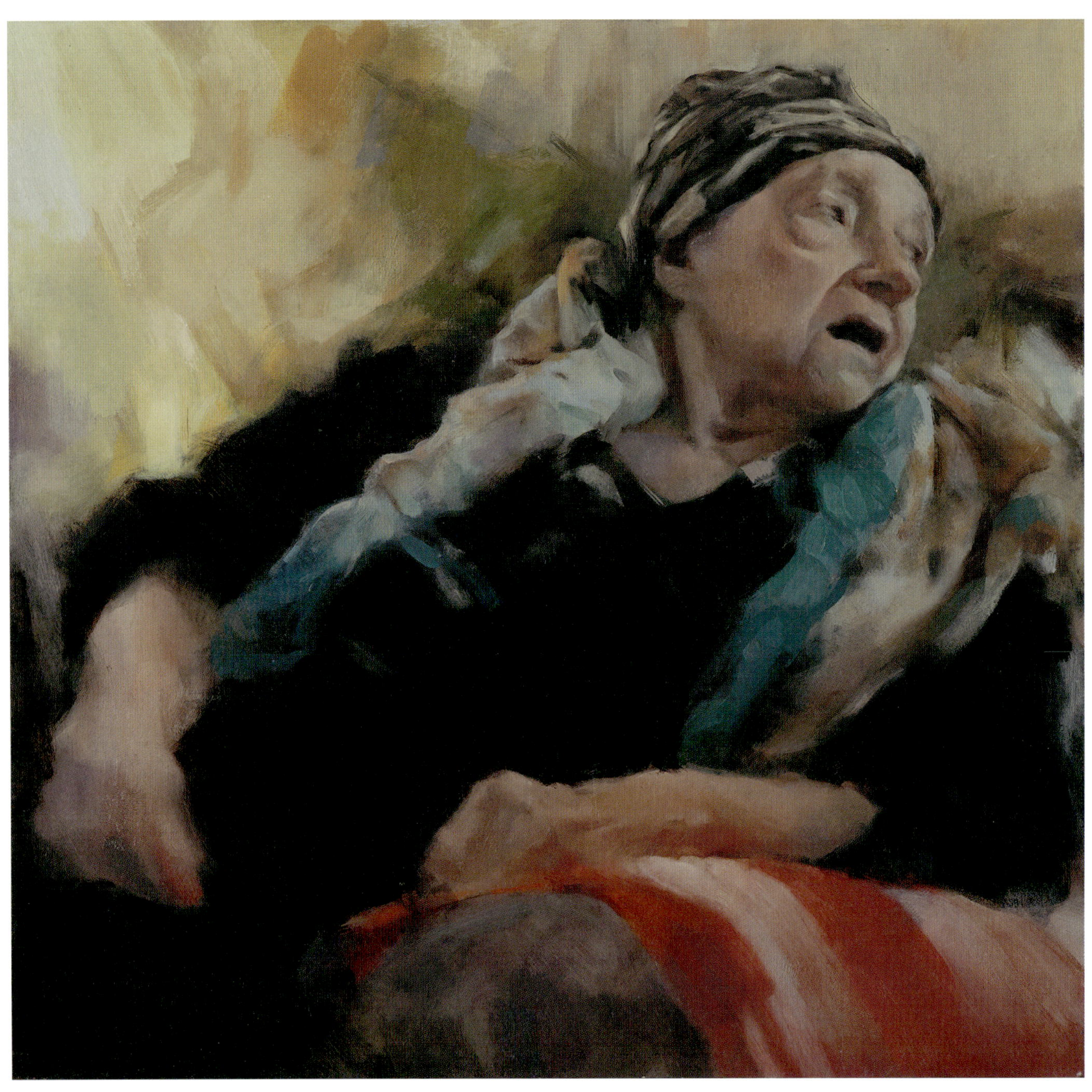

Mick McNicholas
The Artist's Mother, 2024
Oil on aluminium
490 × 490mm

Mick McNicholas represents his 91-year-old mother, Joan. In recent years, he has painted her at every visit, aware that their time together is short. The array of colours and vanishing hands synthesise into a loving yet wistful atmosphere. A wish to connect in a deep and lasting way motivates the creation of these paintings, with observation providing the means for generating a meaningful bond. McNicholas utilises sittings from life and candid photographic studies to create an authentic image.

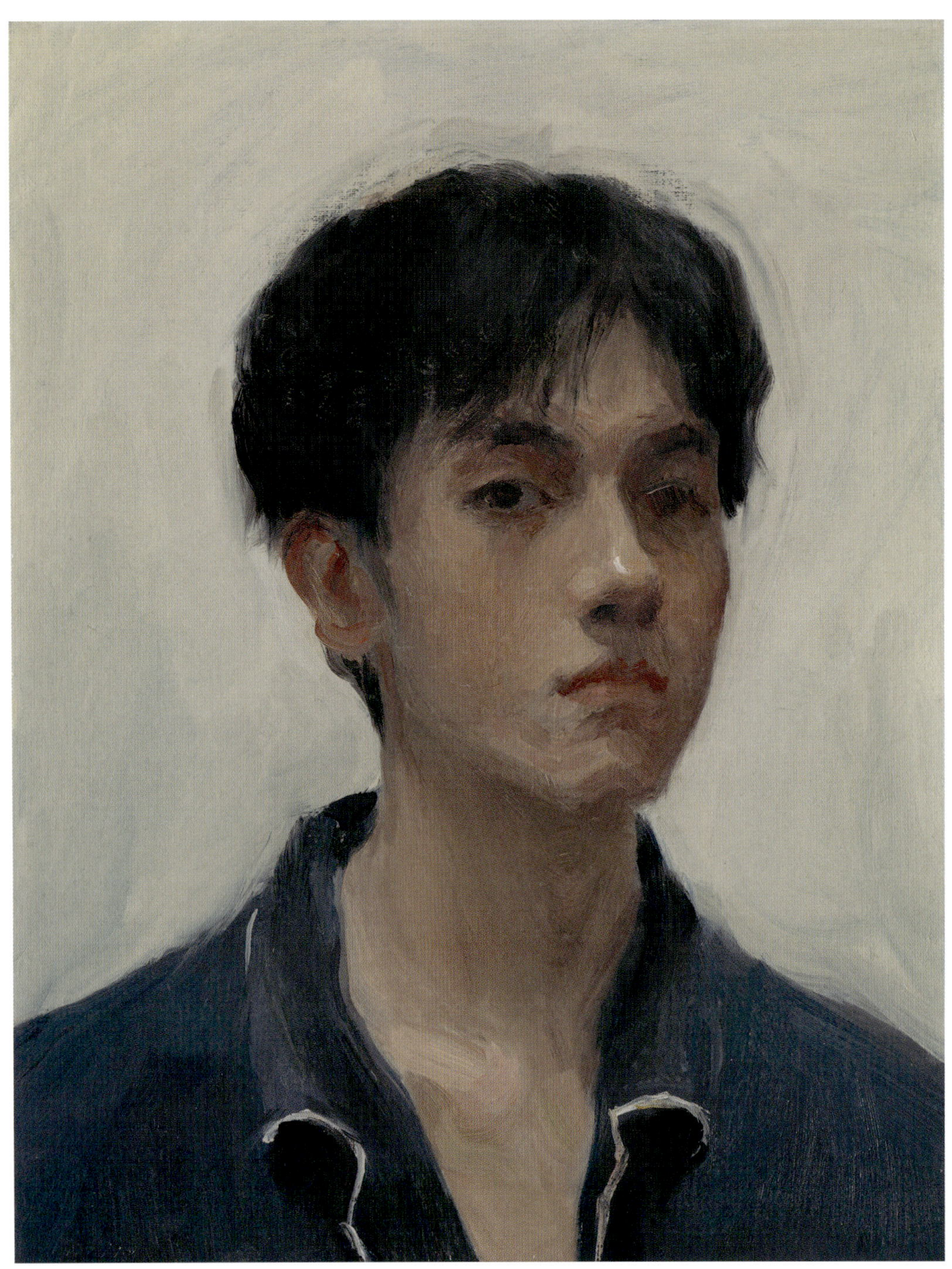

Zaizhu Huo
Wordless: Portrait of Zaizhu, 2024
Oil on canvas
410 × 310mm

Zaizhu Huo is studying at Central Academy of Fine Arts in Beijing, China, and this poetic self-portrait was created while waiting for the results of his college entrance exams. In a moment of uncertainty and disquiet, the artist looked in the mirror and 'tried to see my inner core clearly'. The fluid, waxy substance of the paint, as it runs through the eyes and over the surface of the canvas, seems expressive of this search.

Anca Luiza Sirbu
Chapped Lips and Rain, 2025
Acrylic on canvas
920 × 600mm

Anca Luiza Sirbu's portrait depicts her 14-year-old son, their features defined through a series of incisive and assertive contours. Placed against a grey background representing a rainy sky, the seemingly impassive facial expression and neutral colours conceal a sense of inner tension and stormy rebellion. With each session with her son lasting more than an hour, Sirbu worked hard 'to overcome his stubbornness and grumpiness'.

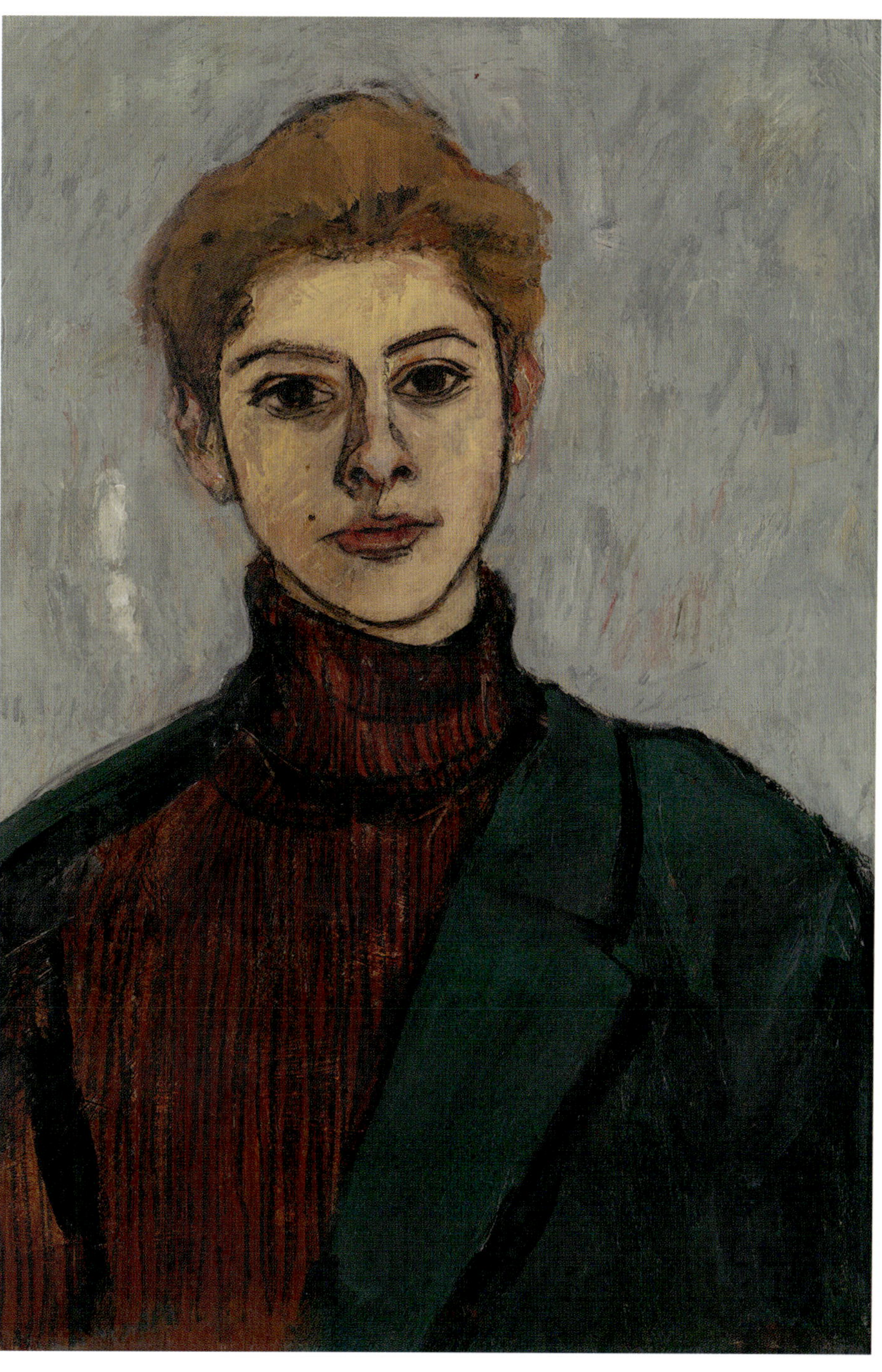

Matthew Midwood
Evelyn, 2024
Acrylic on canvas
760 × 760mm

Motivated by the love of the artist for his subject,
Matthew Midwood paints a portrait of his daughter,
Evelyn. The artist seeks to capture the intentionality
within the tilt of the head and sideways glance, with
which Evelyn returns her father's gaze. Intrigue is noted
within the portrait's unfinished quality, and its provocative
combination of figurative representation and abstract
spatial composition.

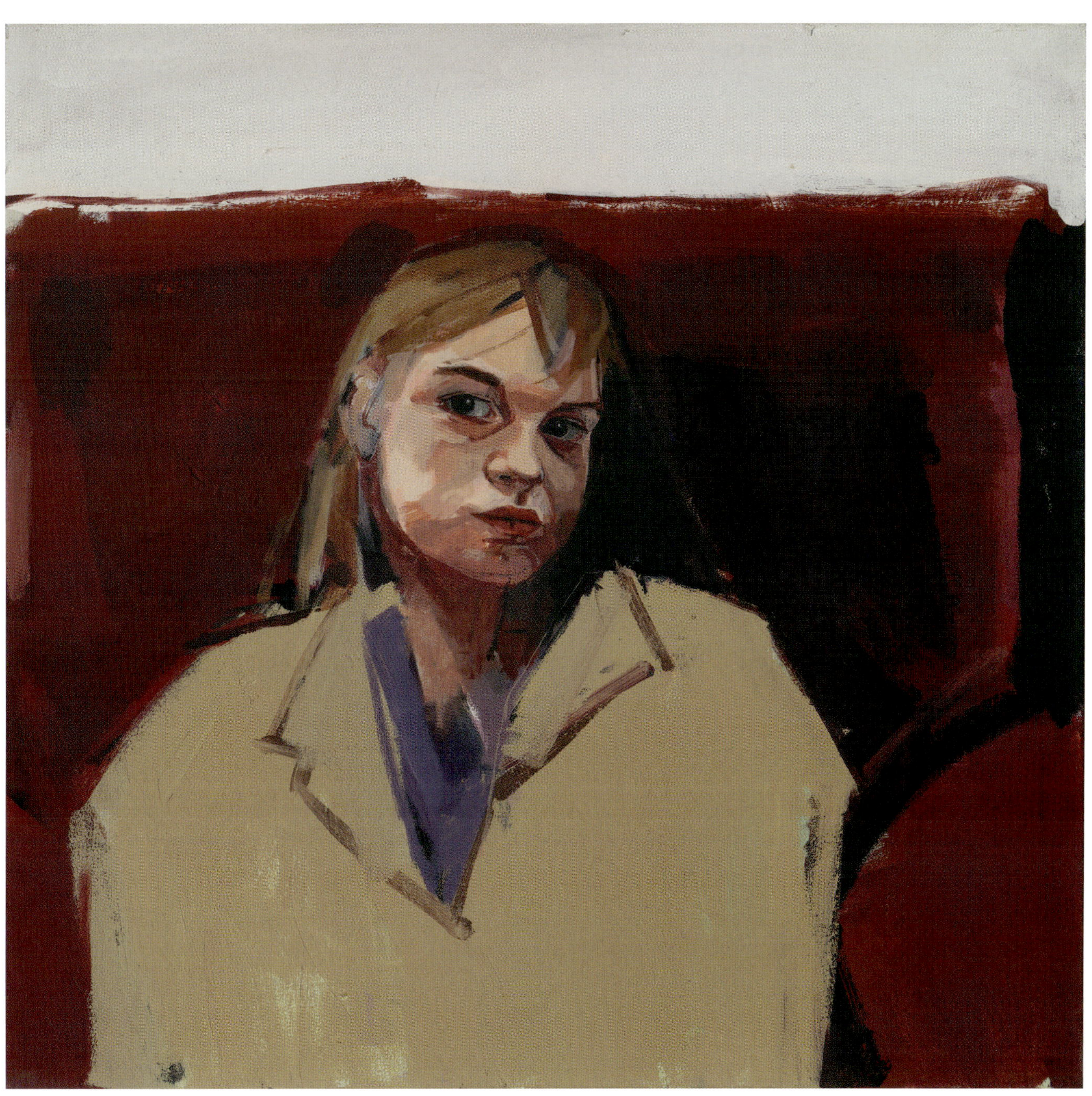

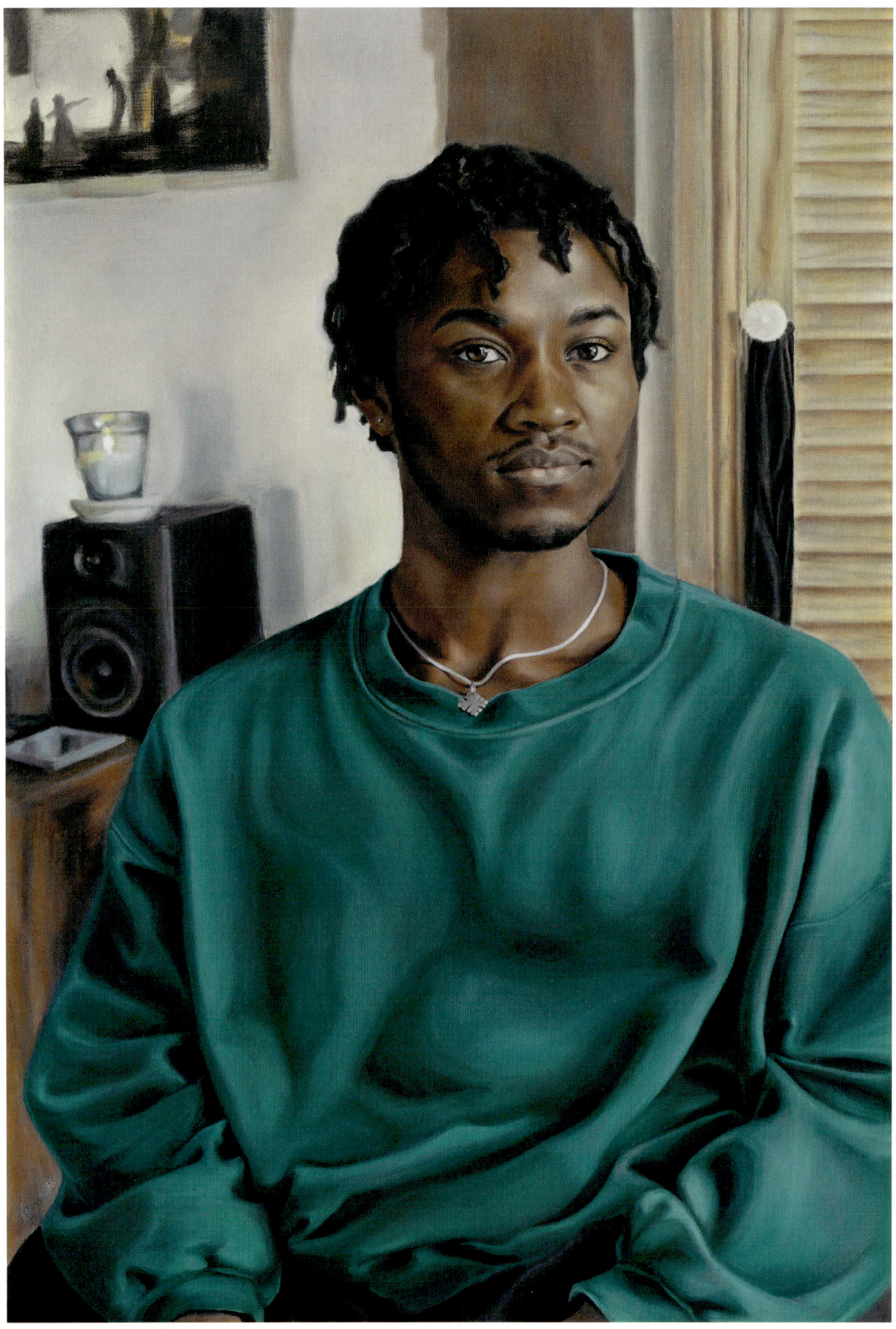

Camila Carlow
Mikael, 2024
Oil on canvas
900 × 600mm

Guatemalan artist Camila Carlow's portrait of Bristol based
photographer and filmmaker Mikael Techane was the
result of a collaborative process. Depicted in the bedroom
from where he works, Carlow aims to capture the sitter's
wisdom, sincerity and identity. Contrasting the deep skin
tones with the teal of the sitter's sweatshirt, the portrait
beautifully reproduces the play of light on surfaces with
the slow and subtle manipulation of translucent oil glazes.

Kevin Kane
Lord and Master, 2024
Oil on board
1200 × 900mm

This striking portrait was created after the artist and sitter met at a charity event. 'Immediately connecting over shared experiences as gay Catholics growing up in suburban Glasgow,' Kevin Kane explores sexuality while referencing the artist and sitter's Scottish connection through traditional wear and Scotch whisky. The books serve as 'meaningful references to our common background and the stories that shaped us.'

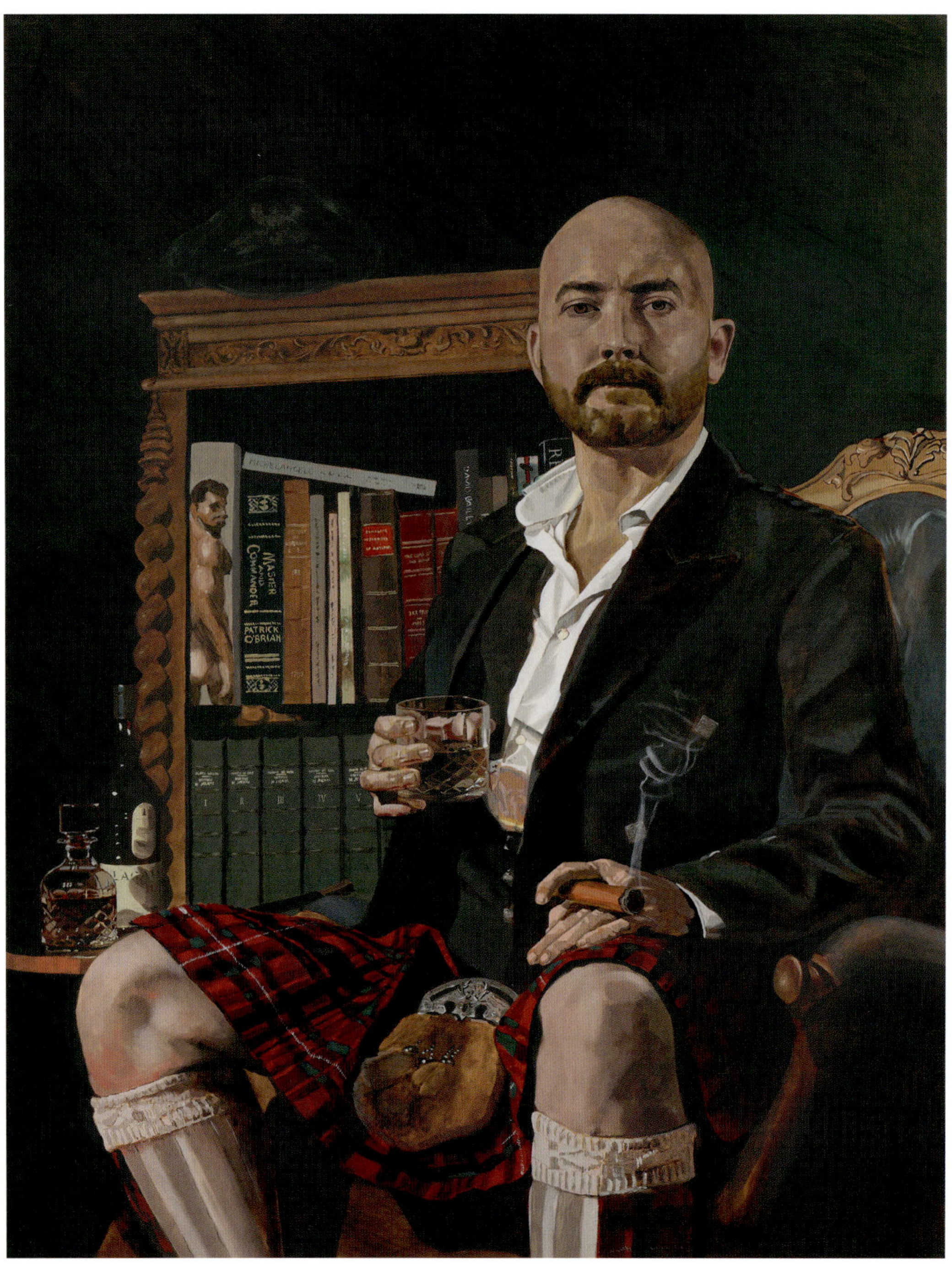

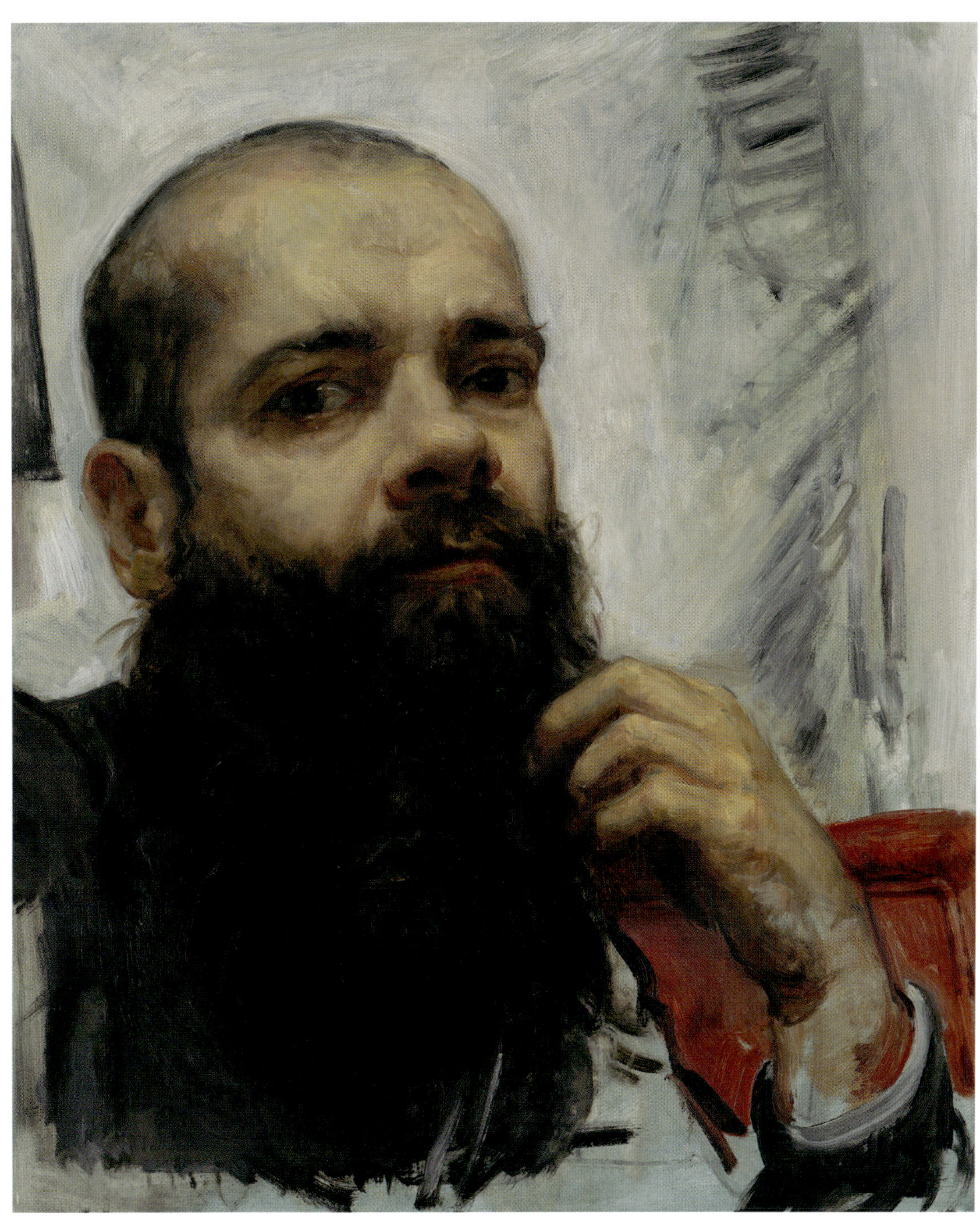

Cesar Santos
Self-Portrait, 2025
Oil on panel
508 × 406mm

This self-portrait by Cuban-American painter Cesar Santos represents an attempt to capture a state of mind. Trained in Miami and Florence, and deeply concerned by the traditions of art history, Santos' work is the result of both contemporary and historical influences. Produced using a mirror, the unfinished quality of the portrait creates a sense of immediacy and connection, as the artist seeks to capture the patterns of his mind through brushstrokes.

Steve Caldwell
Christiano, 2025
Acrylic on board
300 × 200mm

The remarkable focus and meticulous rendering characterises the style of this hyperrealistic portrait by Steve Caldwell. Tight lipped and with narrowed eyes, the sitter seems inscrutable, inspecting us as much as we scrutinise him. Normally a painter of older sitters, Caldwell explains he was drawn to Christiano due to his contrasting youth and willingness to be painted in this uncompromisingly detailed manner: 'I aimed to produce an honest and intimate painting reflecting the sitter's quiet confidence.'

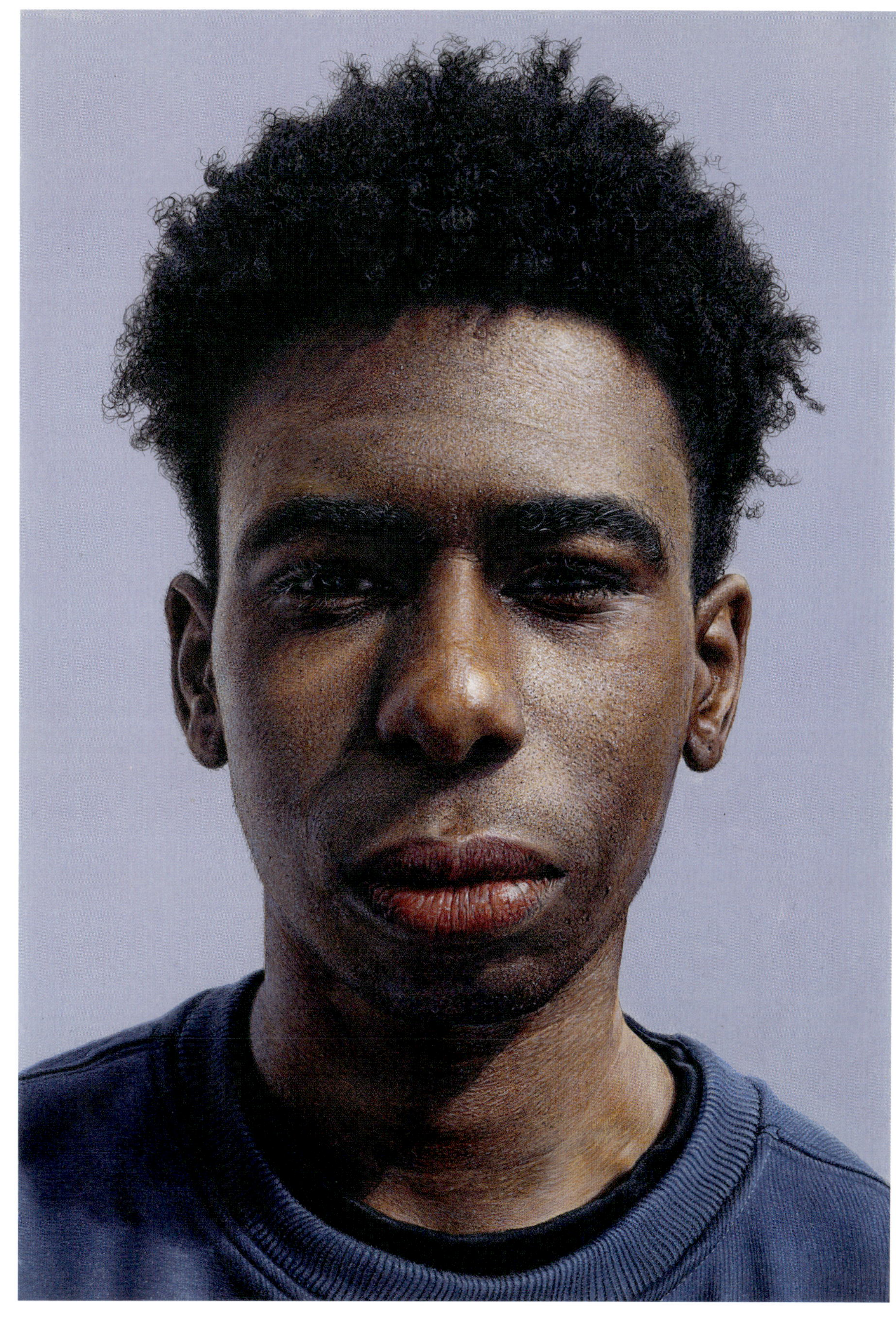

Jo Beer
The Road to Me, 2024
Oil on canvas
560 × 460mm

Max confronts the viewer with a calm, almost
expressionless gaze. Jo Beer depicts Max at the start
of his gender transition journey, using painting as a
way of documentation: 'there is a definite vulnerability
evident in the portrait, and a weight of the long process
that stretches ahead. It is a study of personal choice,
direction of choice and acceptance of choice.'

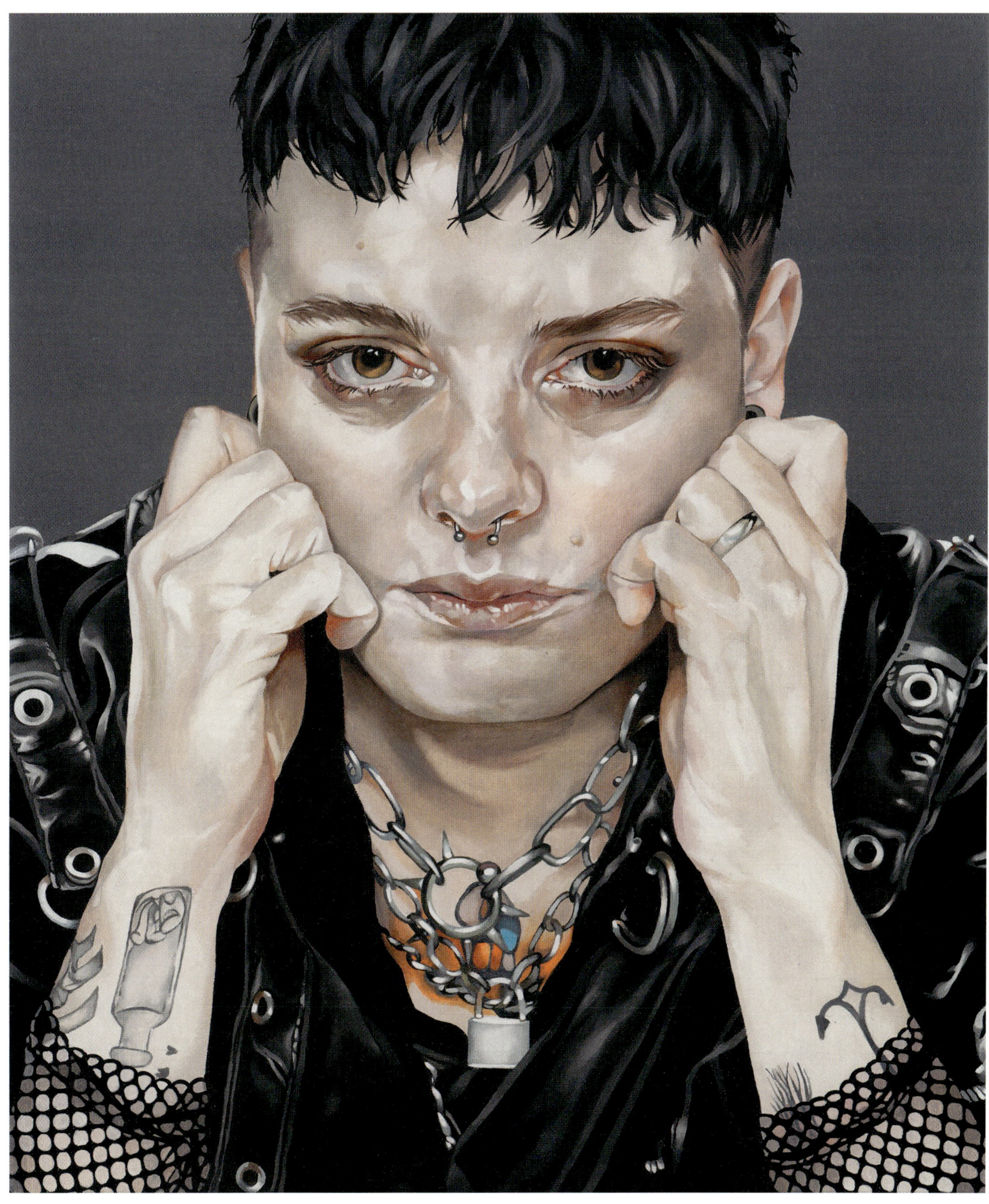

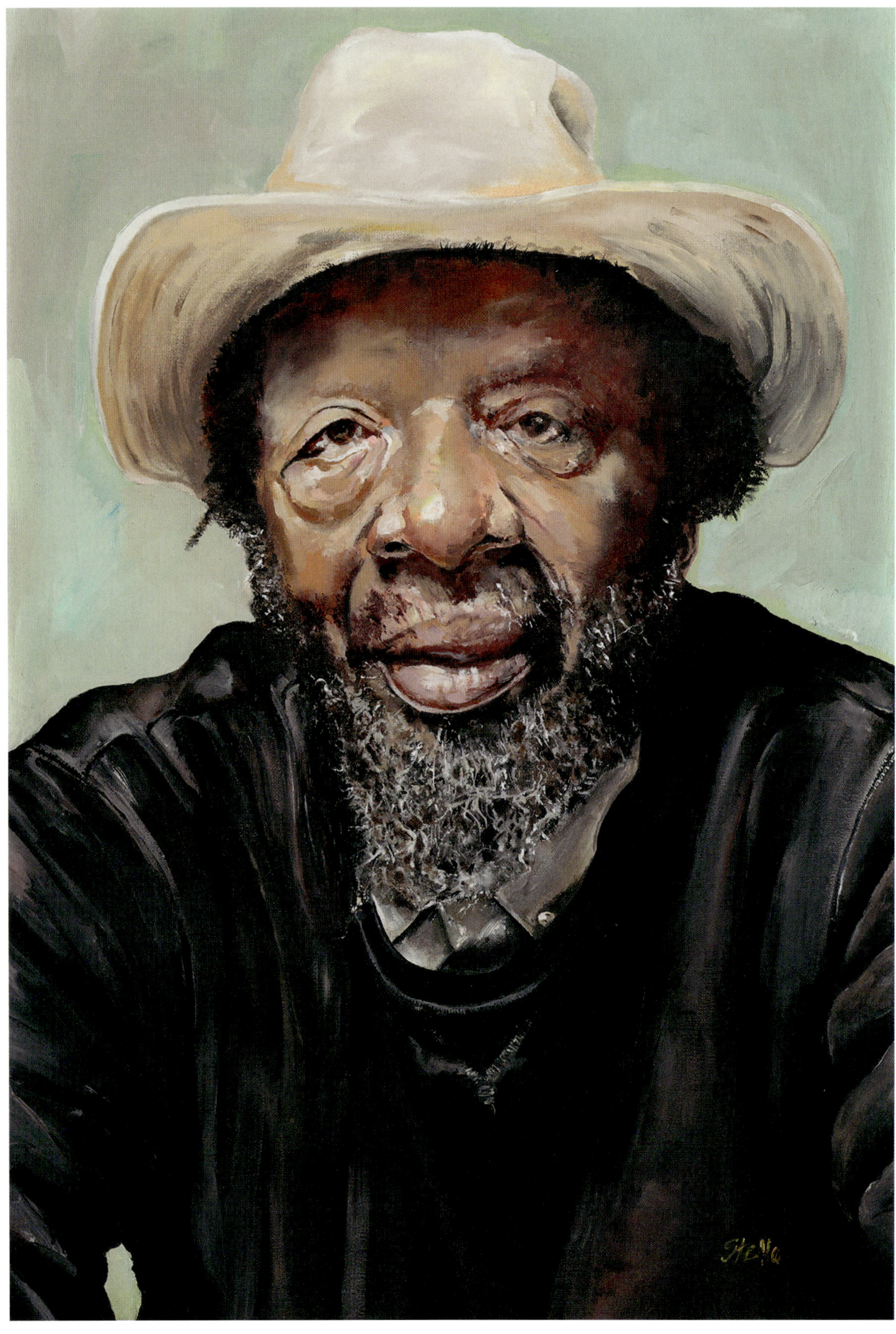

Stella Koureas
Harold, 2024
Oil on canvas
840 × 590mm

In a portrait of her partner's godfather, Harold, Stella
Koureas revels in each aspect of the sitter's appearance.
Deeply expressive and compelling, the artist renders the
folds of the skin, the light on the lips and the depth in
the eyes. Harold has 'an extremely interesting face for a
portrait, I noticed his face almost had a lifetime of stories
to tell', Koureas explains. 'I wanted to capture this and the
calm comforting nature of his personality'.

Nguyen Kim Tuyen
Vu and Sao, 2025
Acrylic on canvas
1300 × 1000mm

Nguyen Kim Tuyen's unique grisaille painting presents skilful mark making and a palette limited to shades of white, grey and black. Created during a period of depression, the restricted colour range is representative of emotions both 'raw and real.' The work depicts the artist and her brother as children, Tuyen seeking to represent the 'children who grew up longing to be heard and understood.'

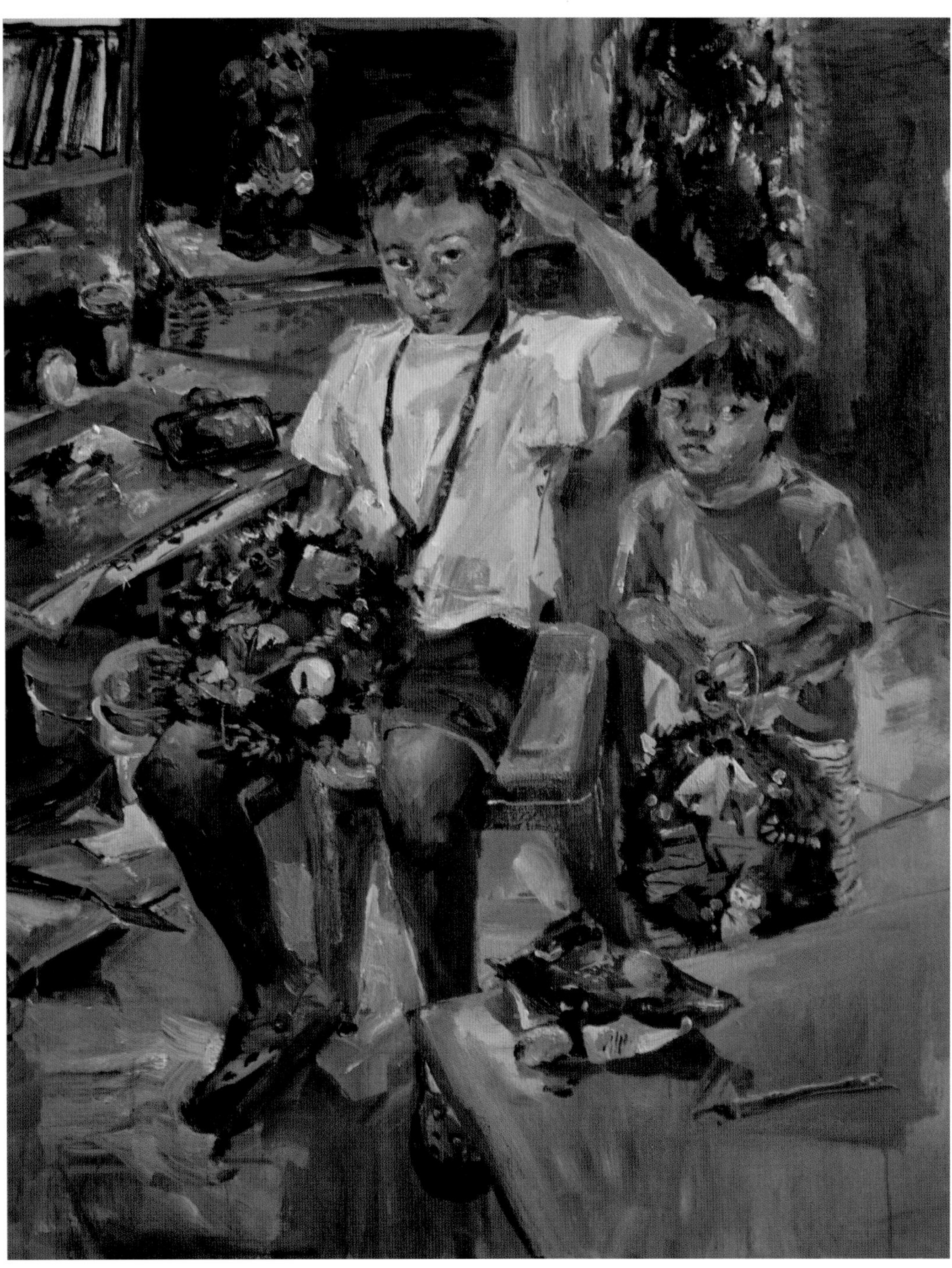

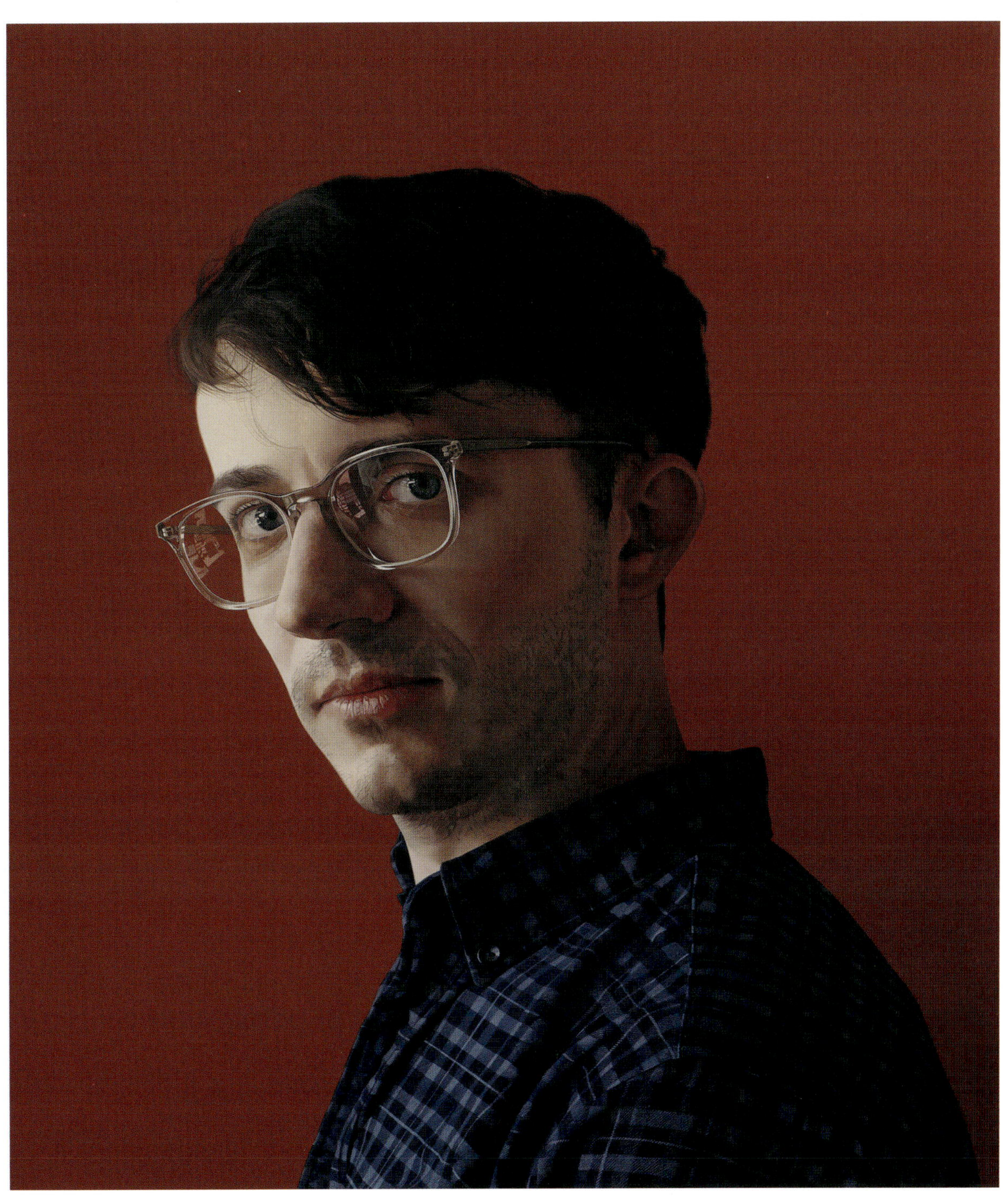

Joshua Waterhouse
James, 2024
Oil on panel
500 × 420mm

Joshua Waterhouse's skilfully painted, hyperrealist portrait is a quintessential *trompe-l'œil* due to its meticulous detail. It is part of a triptych, which includes portraits of the sitter's two brothers, Thomas and Matthew, as commissioned by their father. Head twisted to face the viewer, we see the reflection in James's glasses, their direct gaze as if noticing the viewer walking by.

Dide Siemmond
Portrait of a Sculptor, 2024
Oil on canvas
600 × 500mm

The surface of Dide Siemmond's portrait of the sculptor
Laurence Edwards seems alive with a kinetic, electric
energy. In a Realist style, but exhibiting Cubist influences,
the painting is marked by a graphic use of colour.
The complex spatial composition, from the background
mirror to the looming boot in the foreground, creates a
sense of disorientation. Responding to the sitter's work
and persona, the portrait incorporates maquettes of
Edwards's sculptures and explores 'the messy
plaster-splattered existence of artists in their studios'.

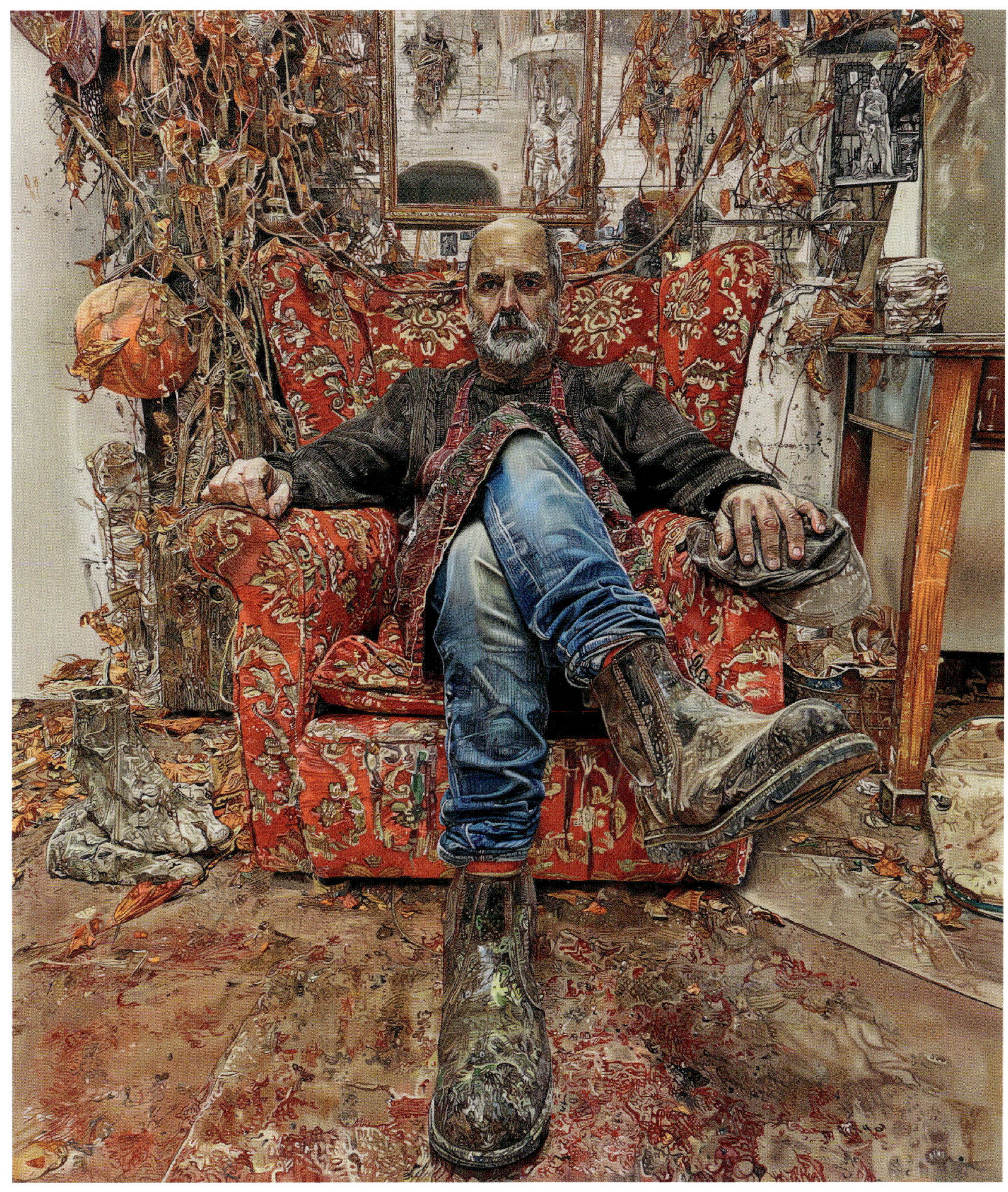

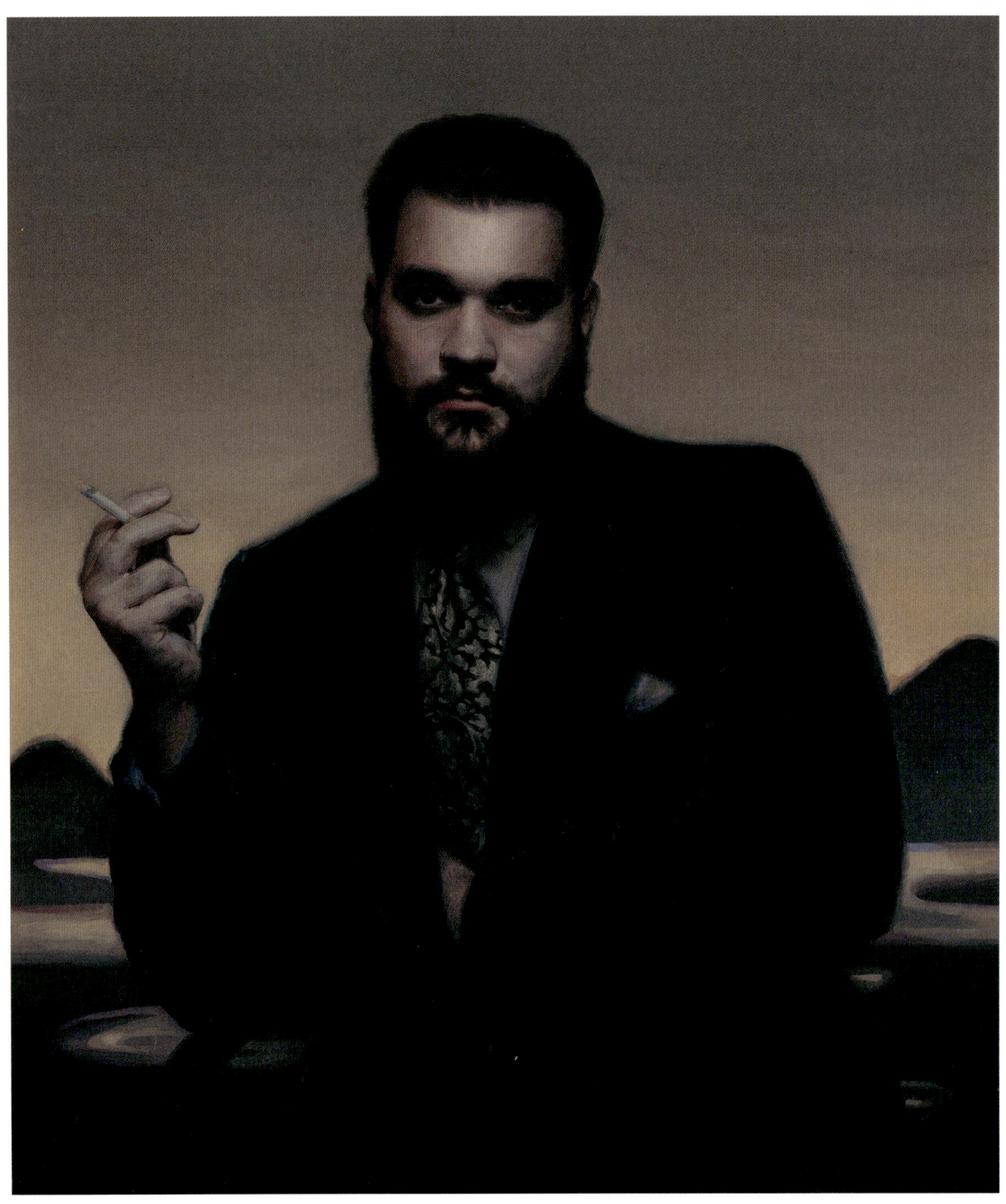

Sofia Welch
Sean After Brockhurst, 2025
Oil on board
610 × 460mm

This witty and charismatic portrait by Sofia Welch represents her fiancé Sean. Painted wearing a dark green velvet smoking jacket, shirt and tie, and set against an abstracted landscape, the sitter holds the viewers gaze with an intense stare. Stylistically evoking the ambience of 1930s, the painting was inspired by the evocative and uncanny portraits by British painter and etcher, Gerald Brockhurst.

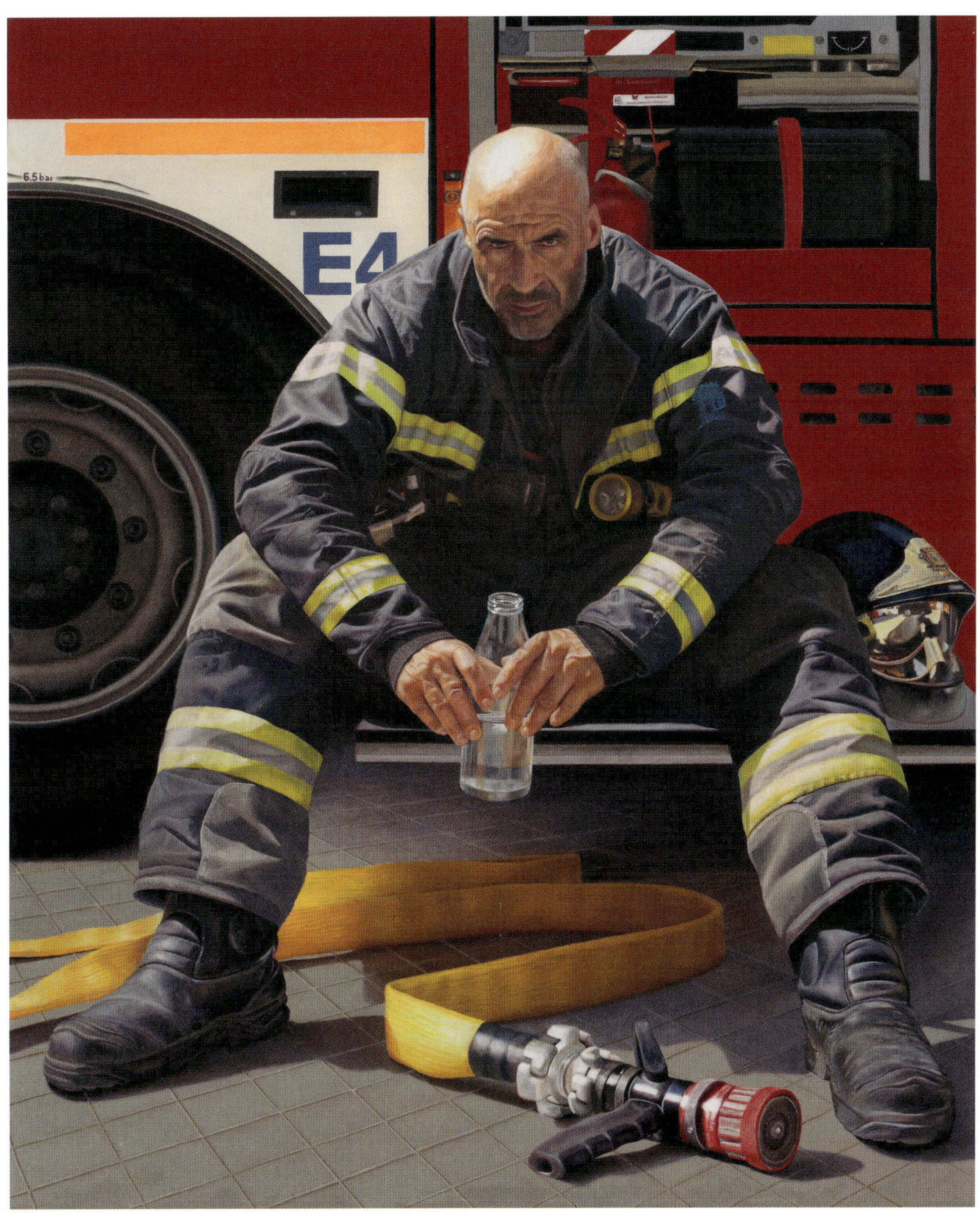

José Antonio Martínez Santos
Satisfaction, 2024
Oil on linen
1500 × 1200mm

Spanish artist José Antonio Martínez's large-scale portrait represents Bruno, his close friend and firefighter. Over 40 sittings, the artist created the artwork on site at the fire station during the sitter's work breaks. *Satisfaction* pays tribute 'to those who give their all to help others.' The sitter's stance is suggestive of historically promoted 'macho' masculinity, which appears in contrast with the care and attentiveness of firefighter duties.

Cassandra Mahoney
*My Mother on her Birthday, the Day
After my Father's Funeral*, 2025
Oil on canvas
300 × 240mm

Cassandra Mahoney explores the complexity of grief in
this portrait of her mother. Familial love and resilience
exists alongside feelings of loss and fragility. An uncanny
domestic scene, with a woman wearing an apron and
blowing out a candle, the artwork is emblematic of its
title: *My Mother on her Birthday, the Day After my Father's
Funeral*. Mahoney manipulates various shades of blue,
successfully enhancing the work's subjective and emotive
quality. The evocative portrait provides little detail in the
sitter's face to 'show the rawness of the emotion she was
experiencing', while the candle light remains a beacon of
'fortitude and hope.'

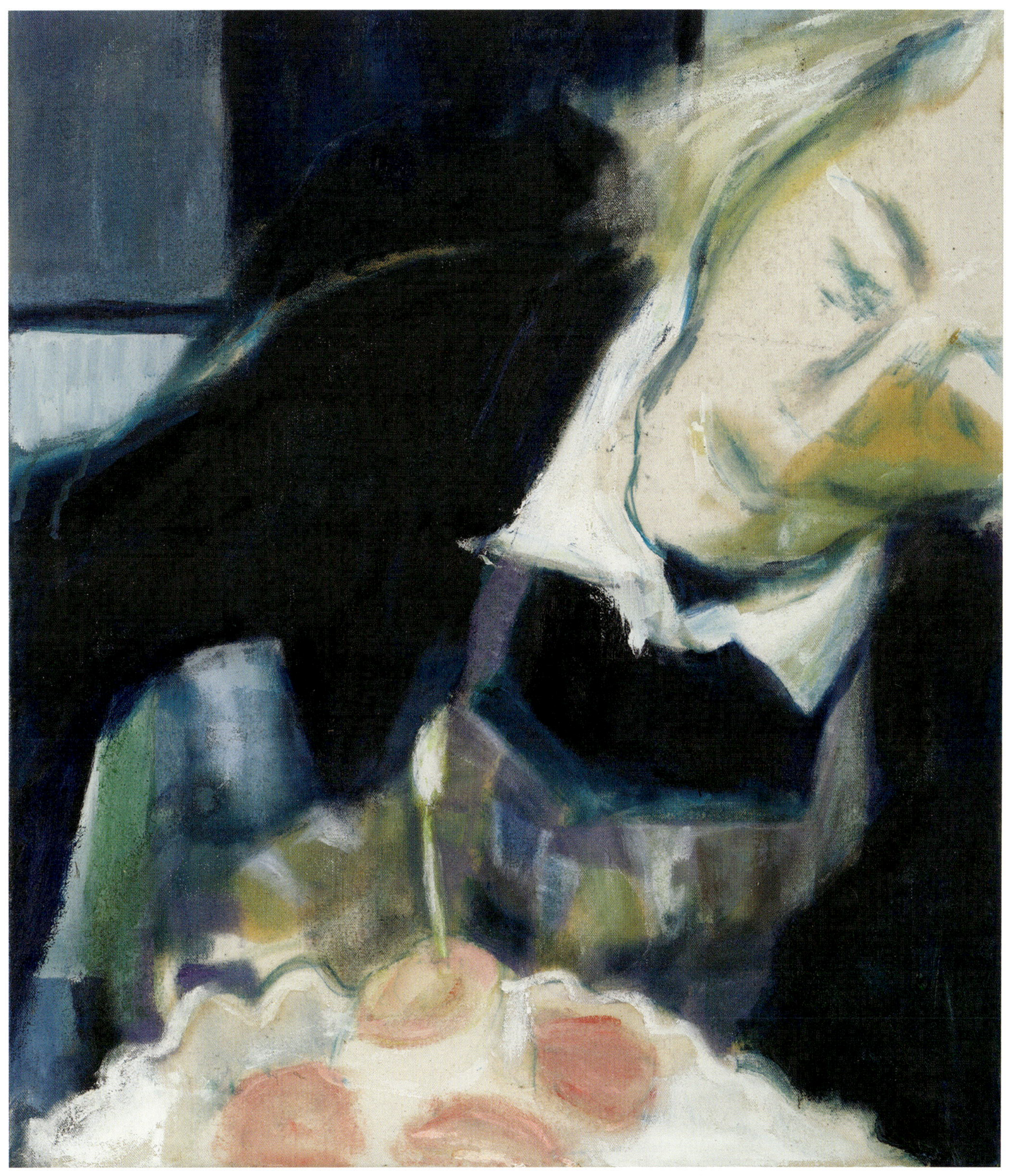

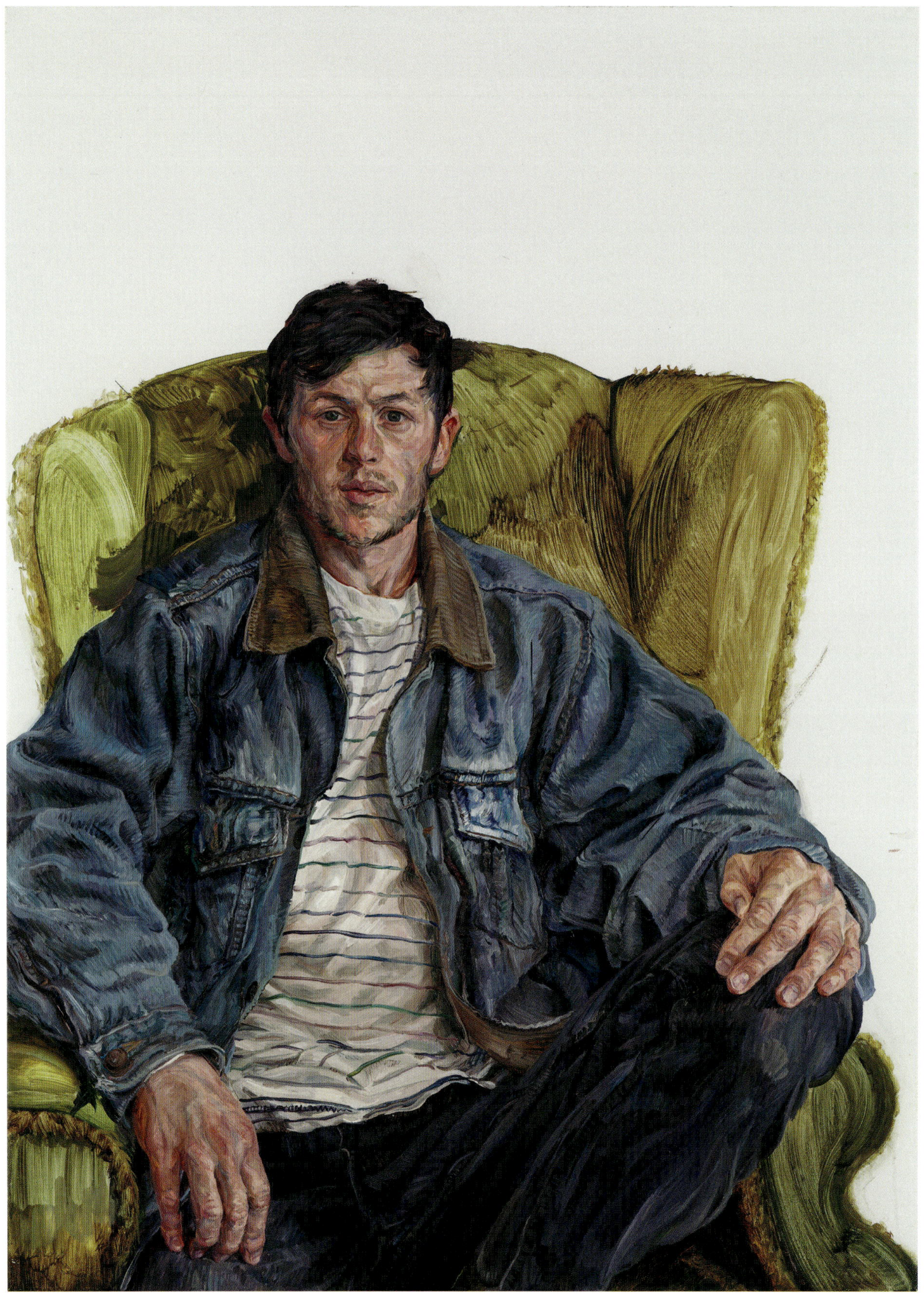

Owain Hunt
Figure in Blue, 2024
Oil on canvas
1100 × 900mm

Dressed in a blue denim jacket and striped t-shirt, staring gently out at the viewer, Owain Hunt's portrait of his old friend immediately expresses the deep sense of connection between artist and sitter. Painted over an 18-month period, the work explores themes of companionship. The deceptively modest portrait speaks to universal themes of the human condition, seen subtly in each individual, articulated brush stroke. The composition places the viewer opposite the sitter as if engaging in conversation; Hunt's work is motivated by the human need to 'invest deeply in relationships and have a shared lived experience'.

Published in Great Britain by
National Portrait Gallery Publications
National Portrait Gallery
St Martin's Place
London WC2H 0HE

Published to accompany the
Herbert Smith Freehills Kramer Portrait Award 2025

Exhibited at the National Portrait Gallery, London
10 July to 12 October 2025

And the Laing Art Gallery, Newcastle upon Tyne
March to September 2026

Every purchase supports the National Portrait Gallery, London.

Information about the exhibition, competition and technical
information can be found at www.npg.org.uk/whatson/
exhibitions/2025/hsf-portrait-award

Cover: *Mikael* by Camila Carlow, 2024

Text on pages 8–15 courtesy Richard McClure

Caption texts written by Amy Emmerson Martin, Contemporary
Curator, and Luke Uglow, Assistant Curator.

ISBN 978 1 85514 800 0

A catalogue record for this book is available from the
British Library.

The Director of the National Portrait Gallery would like to
thank the art handling team, Poppy Andrews, Katherine Biggs,
Sophie Colley, Jessica Daley, Rachel Dunlop, Andrea Easey, Kara
Green, Jahnavi Inniss, Jemma Jacobs, Priti Kothary, Francesca
Laws, Alexandra Lawson, Thulani Maseko, Gráinne McCarthy,
Gavin Nel, Abi Ponton, Skye Redman, Charlotte Regan, Amber
Sherlock, Jude Simmons, Georgia Smith, Liz Smith, Anna Starling,
Eloise Stewart, Anna Sorrell, Benjamin Townsend, Oliver Tratt,
Luke Uglow, Denise Vogelsang, Rachel Whitehouse, Helen
Whiteoak, Rosie Wilson and especially Clementine Williamson,
Exhibitions Manager, Imo Jeffes, Exhibitions Officer, Callum
Brunton, Exhibitions Assistant, and Amy Emmerson Martin,
Contemporary Curator, for their hard work on the project.

Director of Commercial and Operations:
Anna Starling
Publisher:
Kara Green
Production Manager:
Priti Kothary
Project Editor:
Jemma Jacobs
Design:
Peter Dawson, Ronja Ronning, www.gradedesign.com

Origination by Altaimage London

Printed and bound in the UK by Park Communications

This publication is printed on FSC certified paper and has
been manufactured using 100% vegetable oil-based inks and
100% offshore wind electricity sourced from UK wind. Park
Communications Ltd is a carbon neutral production company.

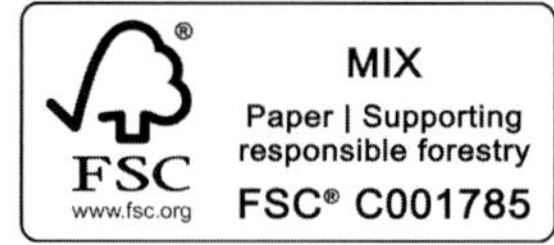